THE LAYMAN'S GUIDE
to EXPERIENCES
——IN——
GOD-REALIZATION

Mark K. Olsen

The Layman's Guide to Experiences in God-Realization
Copyright © 2021 by Mark K. Olsen

All rights reserved. No part of this publication may be reproduced, distributed, or transmitted in any form or by any means, including photocopying, recording, or other electronic or mechanical methods, without the prior written permission of the author, except in the case of brief quotations embodied in critical reviews and certain other non-commercial uses permitted by copyright law.

ISBN
978-1-954932-56-2 (Hardcover)
978-1-954932-53-1 (Paperback)
978-1-954932-52-4 (eBook)

Table of Contents

Home Sweet Home 1
Time to Die 3
Above the Mind 7
The Letter of Truth 9
One is Soul 11
Detachment 13
All is Perfect 15
The Sport of Souls 18
In God's Image 20
Crazy Love 22
Interrupted Discussion 24
Where I'm From 26
Consciousness 27
I Have to Leave 30
Ecstasy 32
Be You 34
All In 37
The Magic Ingredient 40
The Judgment 43
All is Provided 45
Ufo or Ifo 47
Contact 49
Nothing Wrong Here 52

The Catch	55
Recreating the Beautiful	56
The Shadow	58
Meltdown in Pasadena	62
I Can Fly	64
One Cell of the Body	65
The Court of Sat Nam	68
Mind Versus Soul	69
The Narrow Gate	72
Demon	75
The Law	77
Digging for Truth	79
Fifty/Fifty	82
Transcendence	83
What Matters?	85
Death Ward	88
As One	89
Multi-Pointed Consciousness	92
Death Clinic	94
Chacmool	96
E.T.	99
One	103
Flying Fun	105
Worthwhile	108
Paths	110
Visit to Alakh	113

Serpents 118
Little Johnny 120
Upside Down Cake 123
The Music of the Universe 125
A Visit by Agam Purusha 127
Incomplete Bridge 134
Anima 135
The Grand Ball 138
Pinned Down 142
The Appearance 146
Neanderthal 151
Bee Nice 152
Left Luggage 155
Initiations 156
Locked In 164
The Heart of God 166
Mountain Warning 169
The Very Advanced Teachings 170

Introduction

WHEN ONE CONTEMPLATES reading a book on the subject of Spirituality, one naturally may wonder: What are the qualifications of the author?

Does he or she have genuine Spiritual insight to offer, or is it something less: perhaps only simple information, or recycled knowledge that can be found in a million other books. As to qualifications, this author might claim that he is well-educated, that he has studied various teachings for decades, and that he has participated in numerous Spiritual activities, but this hardly qualifies a person to offer deep insight on Spirituality.

What, perhaps, does qualify a person to offer genuine insight into the Spiritual journey? This author would suggest that it is Spiritual experiences. This is especially true in the esoteric tradition–which this author ascribes to–where genuine truth has to compete with a vast wasteland of misinformation and psychic babble. A Spiritual experience does more teaching in seconds than reading and studying may teach in many lifetimes.

Of course this begs the question: What is a Spiritual experience? Some may answer: "What is not?" And they may have a good point! However, for purposes here, a very general definition might be that a Spiritual experience is some kind of a deeper contact with the Power often called God, or the Spirit of God.

A funny thing about Spiritual experiences is that the recipient can take little credit for their occurrence, or boast of any supposed powers or qualifications that led to their manifestation. They are given by the grace of God, or ITS Spirit, and cannot be had for the asking; while one may create the conditions that are conducive for Spiritual experiences to occur, they cannot be induced.

This is the position this author feels himself to be in, having had Spiritual experiences, but with little reason to take a shred of credit for their occurrence. In point of fact, this author resisted Spiritual unfoldment, and needed dragging, while kicking and screaming, into the depths of a greater truth. Paradoxically, although the author believes that Spiritual experiences are a prerequisite for Spiritual wisdom, and that he indeed has had Spiritual experiences, he would resist considering himself an authority on anything. Wisdom is a matter of degree.

However, it is hoped that in the sharing of various Spiritual experiences with the reader, Spiritual concepts and principles will be illuminated, questions will be answered, and inspiration will be given to those striving for greater understanding. Experiences that do not have universal value and validity have been omitted; in addition, other inner events, including initiatory experiences, have been left out or modified lest their secrets preclude seekers from having their own experience and realization.

While the experiences themselves will hopefully illuminate and elucidate major esoteric principles, an extremely brief explanation of esoteric beliefs and practices will behoove those unfamiliar with these teachings, and also those who are familiar with these teachings.

The author assumes that the reader is comfortable with the rudiments of esoteric thought, that there is at least a cursory understanding of reincarnation, karma, and the esoteric tradition. What is the esoteric tradition? Briefly stated: one's true identity is the Divine Self, one cell of God's Spirit-Body, and that over vast cycles of time, one continues evolving towards a more conscious awareness of this identity, bringing one closer to God, and equipping the Divine Self for helping God's cause in some capacity.

There are two very lofty goals that esoteric teachings often revolve around, the first being Self-Realization, which equates to the Christian Salvation, and the second being God-Realization, which equates to becoming one with the Christ Self.

The keystone of esoteric practice and belief is to go inside, and in doing so, find, meet, and merge with one's Divine Self, while living in the physical body on Earth. Esoteric teachings were formerly secret, and passed down orally, but recently, in the last handful of decades, there has been an explosion of Spirituality on planet Earth, and along with it, an explosion of literature on the subject.

Some might think this counterintuitive, but the evidence is everywhere that there has been an increase in Spiritual awareness, and some authorities on Spirituality have gone so far to suggest that the planet has entered a new Golden Age of sorts, or millennium. Of course, if true, this increase in Spiritual awareness on Earth must be balanced, and the negative events and occurrences that balance this increase in Spiritual awareness attract many people's full attention.

Perhaps one of the main reasons for this increase in Spiritual consciousness on the planet is that more highly evolved Souls are incarnating on Earth today, due to the fact that conditions in many places are more amenable to their individual Spiritual growth. To the point: this has created an enormous interest in esoteric paths, and spawned an enormous army of so-called teachers to satisfy this growing interest. Some are good, some are not, and to complicate things, those sincerely wanting information represent many different levels of growth.

It is for this reason that a very brief presentation of esoteric practices may be helpful to those interested. It is this author's hope that most of the suggestions offered on how to follow an esoteric path are universally applicable. However, a stern warning must be given to prospective readers and seekers: the suggestions and thoughts of the author are from his own experience and point of view; as a result, they may radically differ from anything the reader has experienced or believes; total disagreement and disbelief are always totally welcome, and justifiable.

Perhaps one of the first decisions a seeker may face is whether to have a master or *guru*. A genuine master, one who has reached the purely positive planes of heaven, offers tremendous benefits: their instruction and protection are invaluable, especially for the beginning aspirant.

It is important to remember that it is not required; one always has the freedom to choose whether they follow a teacher or not. This is vastly complicated by the difficulty in finding credible teachers; be advised, they are as rare as hens' teeth. However, if one is sincere in seeking a good teacher, one will be directed into the proper channels, either by finding someone highly qualified, or at least one who is familiar with basic concepts and methods needed to begin the Spiritual journey.

Among other things, a master or teacher is a symbol of one's own Higher Self, and whether one uses a teacher or not, the focus should be on developing a communication with one's own Higher Self, and then following Its direction.

Be that as it may, if one is new to going inside oneself, the help of those who are more evolved and experienced is indispensable; additionally, if one is an old hand at going within, and has followed God this way for many lifetimes, the help of those who are more evolved and experienced is indispensable.

This author is indebted to God and ITS channels for everything. However, it bears repeating: the goal is to be a Spiritual adult, self-sufficient and free, leaning on no one but the God within one, and if one wants to follow the God in someone else for a time to help achieve this, or is ready to go it alone, so be it. The Holy Power of God uses many approaches to teach, to help, and to save ITS children.

Perhaps the main thing that differentiates an esoteric path from an exoteric path is the fact that the practitioner is going "within". As the Christ within Jesus repeatedly stated: "The

Kingdom of Heaven is within." One is looking inside themselves, instead of looking to anything outside of themselves.

The practice of "going within" is often referred to as devotions, meditation, contemplation, a Spiritual exercise, prayer, or other terms that denote or connote a combination of stillness and reflection. The purpose of these "exercises" is to still the mind, whether in very short intervals, or for longer periods of time, so that one may receive guidance and truth from higher sources within oneself.

It is a stunning discovery for many to realize that the mind cannot think, any more than a computer can think: all real thinking comes from Soul, and that is why Spiritual exercises revolve around stilling the mind. As the Christian *Psalms* admonish: "Be still, and know that I Am God."

These inner exercises or practices are the heart of esoteric practice: the be all, and the end all, the beginning and the end, the first step and the last; eventually, one's entire life becomes a "Spiritual Exercise."

It must be stressed that there is nothing complex or difficult about going within; it is as natural as smiling at something one finds humorous. Many are either daydreaming, spacing out, or deeply contemplating much of the day; these are all forms of going within.

The difficulty, in the beginning, is in simply doing Spiritual exercises daily; one's mind does not want its owner establishing a closer identity with the Higher Self. Why? Because the mind has a long list of its own desires, and does not want to cede any of its control of the individual to the Higher Self, which cares little about what the mind desires. One could, if they wished, assert that it is impossible for the novice to do Spiritual exercises each and every day, and that assertion would be closer to the truth than its antithesis. The mind is capable and proficient at making the individual too busy to do daily devotions. However, if one is persistent, and is able to successfully do them every day for a number of months, not only do they become an oasis of blissful pleasure and illumination, but exciting things begin to happen: crazy wonderful things!

It is true that to be successful, there is no way around doing them each and every day, the main reason for this being that maintaining a daily contact with one's Higher Self enables It to do everything necessary for one's Spiritual advancement, something that can not be done through the human consciousness without a semi-continuous connection; the human consciousness on its own, without this daily contact with its Higher Self, can do absolutely nothing in the way of Spiritual advancement.

In addition to doing one's devotions daily, one's time involved should be slowly increasing; perhaps one begins with fifteen minutes each morning, and subsequently, after a time, adds an evening "session" of similar length. Perhaps the episodes gradually increase in length of time. One must create and practice Spiritual exercises in one's own way, and at one's own pace. To give further clarity to this vast subject, a brief description of common everyday Spiritual practices will be briefly mentioned, practices that are not only natural and easy, but that anyone can do.

The first Spiritual practice, which is the penultimate of all Spiritual exercises, is also the most unfamiliar to Western students, although this is beginning to change. This practice is simply listening to the sounds of the Holy Spirit within oneself. As the Christ within Jesus clearly states in *John* 3:8, those who have been born of the Spirit can hear the Spirit of God; this is not a metaphor.

This knowledge is common in the East, and is slowly entering the mainstream of Spiritual thought in the West; the *Sikh* religion, several Hindu and Buddhist schools of thought, the *Sant Mat* teachings of Northern India, various Light and Sound paths, such as MasterPath and *Radha Soami* in the United States, are centered around the practice of listening to this "Sound Current" within one. One does not use their physical ears.

And what does one hear? Usually, high frequency pitches, something like the sound that high electrical wires can make; they are created by energies and currents of the Holy Spirit going through one's *chakras* or levels of being, and are heard resonating inside one's head. They are usually subtle and faint, and such a part of one's being that many are not aware that they are hearing these sounds. So much can be said about the wonderful effects that come from listening to these Celestial Melodies: so much that if this practice is new to the reader, the author would recommend the study of a Light and Sound path that features this practice.

Listening to this ineffable music heals, purifies, teaches, soothes, sanctifies, and quiets the consciousness. It is the Audible Sound Current, the Word, the Force, the *Shabda,* the Fountain of God, the Lost Chord, the Flute of Kokopelli, Rumi's *Song of the Reed,* Krishna's flute, the Pied Piper of God, Socrates' daemon, and the elixir of Chinese myth that could unite the *Yin and Yang,* thereby conferring immortality.

There are at least ten major frequencies that can be clearly heard, five from the positive planes of heaven, five from the lower dual worlds, and often times, many minor streams. The Greek pantheon of gods, goddesses, and other mythological figures very accurately personify these various currents of consciousness.

This inexhaustible River of Life is the Holy Word of God and is responsible for creating and sustaining all creation; St. John states: "…without Him was not anything made that was made." One's true name is the chord this euphony of sound makes vibrating through one's being.

Souls conversant with the Astral Plane, the second level of heaven, gain the ability to hear these sounds while living in the physical body, often with the assistance of a teacher who makes the student aware of It. As Soul progresses, a relationship is gradually established with this Audible Stream of Music, and a fantastic thing begins occurring: Soul uses the Sound Current, by increasing its volume at precisely particular moments, to communicate with the human consciousness. This Stream may suddenly come on louder after a random thought or realization, thereby confirming it; It may come on louder just before a contemplated action, thereby warning one against such action; It may come on for any number of reasons, thereby giving one information that would otherwise be unavailable for the human consciousness; It may come on leaving one curious as to why It came on, and sometimes, later through hindsight, one becomes aware of the information's content. Its timing is impeccable; Its wisdom unsurpassed; Its love unspeakable.

One uses intuition to decipher these occurrences, and as the relationship with this aspect of the Holy Spirit grows, one becomes more proficient in intuiting what the communications mean. They are usually patently obvious and the receiver just knows.

If the reader is interested in such lofty goals as Self-Realization, which in the West is often called Salvation or being born of the Spirit, or if the reader is focused on the even higher goal of God-Realization, there is no other way than traversing this Royal Road. In addition, if a teacher, or teaching, has not incorporated a thorough knowledge and practice of listening to this Music of God into their teaching, it is not a high teaching, nor is it a high teacher. Many teachings are found wanting by what they do not know or teach, instead of by what they teach.

One may gain enlightenment through the Light, and eventually gain access to the fourth level of heaven, but this is still within the dual worlds; if one wishes to go further, into the purely positive God Worlds, what the Buddhists term *"nirvana,"* or the Hindu's *"jivan mukti,"* a close relationship with this Sound Current is a necessity. One discovers in time that this Musical Current, this Holy Power, is one's very identity.

Although a totally arbitrary judgment, the second best Spiritual exercise is talking to one's Higher Self. It is certainly not far away; It is closer than one's nose; It is one. Implore one's Higher Self for help; ask It questions; share one's desires and needs; ask or plead for contact and experiences; pour out frustrations and pain; thank It; adore It; worship It. After all, It is one's very Self, and as the great Master Rama taught: *"Paramatman* and *Jivitman* are the same"; Soul in the human body, and Soul as the Divine Self are the same, the difference is in the amount.

If Soul in the human body is compared to a glass of water, the Higher Self is an ocean; but they are both the same water. Sometimes, one may awake, and have the memory of just having had a conversation with some incredible genius on the other side; usually it is one's own Higher Self; there is no better confidant.

A third incredibly powerful practice is Spiritual contemplation. People are contemplating all day; what one contemplates during a Spiritual exercise is the difference. Spiritual contemplation, as defined here, is a reflective process that is a wonderful combination of thinking and not thinking, and during the "not thinking" is when truth may show up.

Contemplating Scriptural passages, or other inspirational works is particularly effective, as Spiritual study primes the pump for Spiritual transmissions, flashes, and realizations. Of course, during a Spiritual "session," one attempts to focus on contemplating the Spiritual side of life, or the Spiritual way of looking at life. Oftentimes, it will involve attempting to translate the latest nudges from the Higher Self into concrete actions on this plane of action, or correct a slight "disturbance in the Force." At other times one may be contemplating the big picture, or asking the big questions: Who am I? Why am I here? Do I have a mission? What occurs after death?

Meditation, which is a close sibling to contemplation, can also be very effective, and is practiced by hundreds of millions of worshippers. Its definition has broadened to cover numerous practices, and many have used it for relaxation, to reduce stress, or perform more efficiently at their job or sports. Its original purpose, to still the mind, has been blurred. Westerners, unused to being still for long periods of time, have had some difficulty in applying it Spiritually.

In this author's experience, there is a very important principle that makes contemplation more effective than meditation, although hairs are going to be split. Nonetheless, by way of explanation: contemplation sets the table, but does not know what meal is going to be served; meditation, as practiced by many paths, sets the table, and focuses on receiving a known meal.

Frankly, the latter may not work as well. It is difficult to force something from the Spiritual Forces as the Holy Spirit decides the menu, and It is not directed by man's will. As Paul's letter to Ephesus points out: the Christ does things "according to His good pleasure, which He hath proposed in Himself." Successful contemplation does not focus on a goal, or concentrate: it "unconcentrates." It does not assert its will: it is relaxed and natural, and gently invites Soul's whisperings and direction, while serenely drifting in and out of thought on a particular subject; it is the "out of thought" time that makes it Spiritual contemplation, and this is precisely when the truth may present itself.

It is known that Spiritual communications are often so very subtle, and are a "still small voice"; both Spiritual contemplation and Spiritual meditation can enable one to hear It. The keystone to success in both is stillness of mind. Stop thinking; know everything.

An additional powerhouse of Spiritual athletics is the visualization of Spiritual subjects in the imagination, or one's third eye. This practice is rather self-explanatory as it is done regularly by all alive in the human body; people think in pictures.

The visual equivalent of listening to the Sound Current, it is a wonderful aid to arresting thought, and is also often used in techniques involving out-of-body travel. It is generally agreed that visualizing one's Master is the highest subject one can choose; if one has no master, visualizing one's Higher Self is particularly apropos; after all, meeting and merging with one's own Higher Self, is one way of stating Soul's prime goal.

Chanting is also a wonderful technique to center oneself and induce desired moods and feelings. Many chant specific mantras that have been very carefully constructed to harmonize with various energy centers within one's body. Others chant the names of their god, or their savior.

It is also effective to customize a mantra to fit a situation, and one may find that after a few hundred repetitions, its message begins sinking in. Simple repetitions such as "I love you Father," or "please be with me Spirit," or, "thank you Mother," or, "help me "Savior," are also very effective. Some feel that chanting is a beginning technique, and that there comes a time, when one has indeed centered themselves, that it naturally stops with the practitioner hardly being aware of it; others chant their entire life. Prayer is also a simple way to go within. The *Christian Bible* instructs one to "pray without ceasing," and Jesus admonishes his followers to "enter into thy closet…shut thy door…" and "pray to thy Father in secret." Muslims are asked to pray five times a day.

These simple practices, and countless variations of them, are all one needs to contact the Higher Self, and one's own Spiritual practices should be customized to exactly the way that the seeker desires to do them. This is all it takes to be successful at an esoteric path; the Holy Spirit, and one's Higher Self, do the rest.

Doing these exercises daily opens the door to incredible riches that can not be exaggerated. After a time, there is a progressively increased clarity of communication with one's Higher Self, and it is possible for It to communicate anything wished to the human consciousness, be it through a dream, by way of a vision, through a voice inside one's head, a sudden flash, a sign or omen, or by use of the Sound Current. One cannot predict or limit the Holy Spirit.

An important point is that as wonderful as it is to keep one's attention intermittently on higher things during the day, it is not a substitute for concentrated Spiritual exercises that are free from all distractions. There is a process developed by the aspirant whereby the Higher Self becomes present to a much higher degree during scheduled "sessions" with one's Higher Self; the two together, incidental and scheduled, are both required.

Slowly, step by step, this relationship grows closer and leads to further experiences, eventually resulting in actual contact with the Divine; this kindles the love nature into a roaring fire, and the desire to pursue God increases dramatically. *Paramahansa* Yogananda gave a wonderful answer to a person who questioned him on how to love God. He said: "My poor friend, you have not had any experiences with God. When you have had an experience with God, you will not have to ask how to love Him."

This is so true: any contact with the Divine sets one's Spiritual hair on fire. As is true in any pursuit, one's success in developing further rapport with the Divine will be commensurate to their sincerity, effort, and evolutionary capacity: a successful classical musician usually practices from six to eight hours a day.

These "sessions" with one's Higher Self should be done alone, free from distraction, and in an environment conducive to reflection: one should be relaxed and comfortable. It does not matter how one sits; it does not matter how one breathes; it does not matter if one's back is straight. What does matter is where the attention is placed, or not placed during the exercise. Everything else is an incidental. Krishna states: "When he completely withdraws the senses from their objects, as a tortoise draws in its limbs, then his wisdom is steady."

Hopefully, the brief preceding description of esoteric practices has helped dispel confusion about practicing an esoteric path. It is simple, natural, and does not require any special knowledge, contrary to what many paths would have people believe. It can be practiced anywhere, at any time, and by anyone. And fellow Souls, be persuaded: if one faithfully spends quality time doing such described practices each and every day, customizing them to fit one's own preference, Spiritual experiences will be assured: guaranteed.

One's Higher Self is not trying to hide from one: quite the reverse. The following Spiritual experiences presented are a combination of several different kinds of experiences: various types of sleeping dreams; waking dreams; visions; out-of-body experiences; mystical happenings; miracles; initiations, and other happenings that are difficult to classify. "In a dream, in a vision of the night, when deep sleep falleth upon men, in slumberings upon the bed; Then He openeth the ears of men, and sealeth their instruction,…" (Job 33:15,16) A book in itself could be written about some of these experiences, so lofty and poignant are the truths presented; however, this author hopes to be selective and dwell briefly on the broader points.

Of course the readers are encouraged to interpret and analyze these shared experiences for themselves; many will see more insightfully than this poor aspirant can see. The beginning experiences related are from this author's own beginning journey into the inner worlds so many years ago.

Home Sweet Home

IT WAS ANOTHER hot, humid, April morning in Nha Trang, Viet Nam, and after serving guard duty the previous night, I was returning to my hooch, anxious to take a nap before it got too hot. I had four months to go in my tour of duty, and like most GIs in Nam, I was lonely and homesick. Too tired to take off my boots, I laid back on my bunk in the hooch, and longingly thought of home, (the "World" in GI parlance) and for consolation, I decided on a whim to imagine that I was in the backyard of my childhood home in Minnesota. I pictured myself reclining on a lounge chair in the Sun, basking in the warmth of home and hearth, and all that it represents. I began to imagine all the details of our backyard: there would be the hedge to my side, and yes, the big spruce was right in front of me, the garden to the far side would be bare at this time.

Oooooh! the Sun felt so good and everything was feeling so real, so relaxing, when suddenly, my mother came out the back door of the house, sauntered slowly over to the clothesline, and began hanging up what appeared to be some kind of knitted creation! I was shocked! Startled! Thunderstruck! I hadn't imagined her in my fantasy, yet there she was, as real as could be. I sat up out of my reverie on the bunk with a start! This was too amazing. This was disturbing.

I was virtually positive that what I had seen could not be reality, that it was some trick of the imagination, but after contemplating the matter, I decided it wouldn't hurt to write my mother a letter, and rather innocuously ask her if she had hung anything on the clothesline that particular day. It took two weeks to get her reply, one week for mail to travel each way, and her answer unsettled me.

Among other things she wrote: "When I got your letter asking me if I'd used the clothesline on April third, I laughed out loud. No person hangs clothes outside in Minnesota during the month of April. But then for some reason I remembered, that was the day I had washed a knit scarf in the sink, and since it was an unusually warm, sunny day, I hung it on the clothesline outside for fear the dryer would shrink it."

My mother never asked me why I had asked about the incident, seemingly oblivious to the implication that I had somehow known she had hung something on the clothesline that day. However, it was not lost on me what had happened, and it kicked around in the back of my head, even though I resisted thinking about it.

Comments: This was the first experience I had that was completely divorced from the realm of "normal" experience, and it left me in a kind of shocked limbo; my mind did not want to believe it, but at the same time, what had happened was undeniable. Funny thing: we pray for miracles but when one occurs the mind does not want to believe it. Somehow, I had been out-of-body, viewing an incident twenty thousand kilometers away, and there was not a reasonable explanation that I could come up with and believe.

As I came to understand later, my intense longing to be home certainly played a key role in making it happen. This experience began breaking up old thought forms and paradigms, compromising my conditioning about how life is. Sometime later, when back in the United States, I began reading literature on various schools of thought, and chanced across a book featuring out-of-body travel: I was ready to believe it possible, and with my interest piqued, I dove into the world of esoteric literature. Within a short time, I became curious enough to begin digging more deeply, and I began doing Spiritual exercises. All heaven broke loose.

Time to Die

AFTER I HAD been doing daily Spiritual devotions for several months, I had a very clear dream. In the dream, I was laying in a field of brilliantly colored flowers next to a bald old man. I appeared to be a boy of about seven years old, and the old man looked to be seventy or so, although he appeared strong, quiet, and confident. The field of flowers stretched as far as one could see, and the sparkling colors were so vivid and bright that avalanches of hue seemed to be shimmering around us. Many of the colors were new to me.

The flowers appeared conscious and were looking at us, curious as to who we were. They were joyous and proud of their beauty, and their very consciousness seemed to be a love of life. Intoxicating fragrances that kept changing, each bouquet seemingly better than the last, drifted right through us, as though mere bodies could not prevent their diffusion.

The old man looked at me and calmly stated: "It's time to die."

I was not entirely shocked, but resistant, as though this had been discussed before, and I asked him, "Is it really necessary?"

Without any change of facial expression, he barely nodded, "Yes."

"Oh please," I pleaded, suddenly overcome with the gorgeous scene surrounding us, "please, just give me thirty more seconds so that I can look at these flowers. Please! Just thirty seconds more, please!" The thought of dying and leaving this incredible field of beauty behind me was simply too unbearable to imagine.

Comments: When I had this dream, I was not Spiritually old enough to comprehend it. The message seemed a bit hazy: after several years on my journey for further understanding, it became quite clear. Some would describe the dream as archetypal, not only because death in the Spiritual life is such a common archetypal motif, but in the sense that it was referring to my entire Spiritual journey; it was not a one-time occurrence of the moment.

Naturally, it was easy to appreciate the dream's more obvious message, that dying and leaving beautiful things behind is painful, but I had little idea of how extensive the crucifixion of the personality was going to be, and how necessary that it would be to Spiritual growth.

Souls know this; they aren't stupid; they have lived forever. And that is one reason why very few go "all in" on a Spiritual path: they inwardly sense that it means progressively giving up their worldly desires, and they, being identified with the mind, think *mammon* looks better than God. Buddha reportedly said that these worldly desires were the source of all pain. James, in the *Christian Bible* agreed and stated that it was these desires, not God's tests, that were the source of human problems. Krishna is direct about the subject: "Renounce all enjoyments and pleasures, offer gifts, chant My name, undertake vows and practice austerities. Do all these things for My sake alone."

This dream was a cautionary tale of sorts, and the old man, who was representing my Higher Self, was the harbinger of my Spiritual future. An interesting aspect concerning Spiritual "death," is that the individual, as the personality, does not die or self-surrender willingly. The ego, and the human mind of which it is a part, will not "kill" themselves; it would be like asking a fish not to swim. The Holy Spirit leads one, step by step to the chopping block, teaching one the futility and illusion of one's petty little desires, removing them one by one, while at the same time unveiling the beauties and rewards of the Spiritual life: freedom, love, wisdom, power, joy, contentment, and a virtual cornucopia of additional wonderful things.

People always do what they want to do, always, and the Holy Spirit, and the Higher Self, never force one to do otherwise. When a seeker decides to take another step forward, leaving the old behind, it is always because one desires to. The first gigantic death, after innumerable little ones, comes either just before, or just after the beginning of Self-Realization on the fourth plane of heaven, and is the dark night of Soul that St. John of the Cross so dramatically writes of. One's lower identity has its bluff called, and the time has come to find out in much greater depth that the human personality is powerless, stupid, helpless, weak, foolish, selfish, and any other negative character traits that one cares to mention. It is time for the seeker to more fully identify with the Higher Self, which will eventually lead to complete Self-Realization on the fifth plane of heaven.

This experience is attended to by an enormous increase of awareness and consciousness, as the seeker, within certain parameters, has met and merged with the Higher Self and Its consciousness: ... "he is a new creature: old things are passed away; behold, all things are become new." There is an interesting irony that attends the Salvation experience: due to the fact that one can "see" as never before, one perceives, among other things, the tremendous flaws in their own personality, problems that are deeply hidden and unconscious: in some respects, the work on purifying themselves has just fairly begun.

One might think that the death at Self-Realization is the final one, but for those who journey further, the deaths, or purifications, occur at every major initiation, and they are more intense, not less, as every false identity of the Soul and the human personality is ripped away. This culminates in the "Passion of the Christ," which occurs at God-Realization, involving the inheritance of one's Christhood, and the meeting and merging with one's Divine Self.

Lest this talk of personality death sound too grim, one must remember, for every false illusion and lower identification removed, one's identity as Soul grows much stronger: old fears are vanquished, a new serenity is established, old problems are solved, new attitudes take hold, old hurts are removed, a new joy and love explodes forth, old limitations are erased, and new freedoms are found, including the freedom from one's own ego. In addition, Soul has reentered the "Garden of Eden," eaten from the "Tree of Life," and gained a new level of immortality.

There is a logical parallel to the Spiritual death motif: while those committed to the Spiritual life have become dead to the world, those pursuing the worldly life are dead to Soul. Jesus showed little sympathy for the gentleman, who before following Jesus, wanted to bury his father: "Let the dead bury their dead."

D.H. Lawrence, in his famous poem, "We are Transmitters," refers to them as the "living dead."

Recently in Tinsel Town, there has been an explosion of movies, television shows, and books about zombies. It is small wonder as Earth is overrun with them, and not only have they died to their own Higher Self, they attack others who have not been infected. In the big picture, there is nothing wrong with this. These Souls are simply at a stage where their identity is fused with the mind, instead of their Higher Selves. This will all straighten out in time; one does not criticize children for being fascinated with toys.

Above the Mind

THIS EXPERIENCE ALSO occurred early in my journey. In a clear dream, I, my partner and daughter, and the entire planet of Earth, had been captured by aliens from another galaxy, and the invaders were subsequently testing everyone before sending them to an appropriate job somewhere in their vast system of planets. We had been taken to an enormous building, and I had been separated from my wife and daughter for the exam.

After finishing my test earlier than the others in the room, I began exploring the large building we had been transported to. After a bit, two lab technicians in white coats caught up with me and explained that since I had totally aced the first test, I needed to take another more advanced exam.

The second exam was only five questions, and dealt with lengthy, obscure equations. I quickly wrote down the answers, which seemed to amaze the technician administering the test. He looked over my answers and said: "Well, you got them all right, but how did you do them so quickly? Please show me just how you figured the first one out."

I looked down at the first problem. It was a long equation, riddled with letters in brackets over other numbers that were squared or cubed in parentheses, multiplied times other figures that were circled with unrecognizable symbols and letters that I had never seen before.

There was no way I could mentally do this: I looked up at the doctor and said, "Where I come from, we use a system above the mind."

"Above the mind?" he questioned in surprise, as though he had never heard of such a thing. He very slightly nodded to a nurse standing near the wall and she flipped a switch, turning on a globular light near the ceiling above my head.

I suddenly felt the top of my head grow warm, and I looked at the doctor and rather disdainfully asked: "Brain scan?" as though it was totally futile to try finding anything worthwhile with such an archaic instrument. He looked away as though he had been caught doing something embarrassing.

Comments: The planet Earth adores the mind, and one constantly sees and hears intelligence being worshipped; one seldom hears a word about wisdom. Some of the smartest people on the planet do not even believe in God: so much for their intelligence.

However, their lack of belief is very understandable: the creation is so vast and incredible that it is too big for their little brains to conceive of. How does one conceive of quadrillions of galaxies on the first plane of heaven, which is a tiny fraction of the plane above it, and that plane of heaven a tiny fraction of the one above it, and so forth on up with uncountable levels?

The mind when attempting to conceive of God, has the same chance a flea has of inventing a nuclear device. It seems counterintuitive but the mind is unconscious and cannot inductively think: it is true that sense perceptions, stored memories, conditioning, motor movements, and emotions give the impression of thinking, but thinking it is not; it is just hardware and software.

This is not to impugn the wonderful value of having a computer, and one of its greatest functions is that it can be trained to be put on receiver mode, so to speak, or standby, and register communications from Soul. Then its other functions come to bear: analyzing what one has received and applying it to one's life. The mind cannot inductively think and Soul doesn't have to; It just knows.

The Letter of Truth

A SUBSEQUENT DREAM HAD me standing along side a table in a large library. Seated at the table was a young girl, and she was worried. She had a very important exam coming up that if passed, would license her for a prestigious position. She looked up at me with pleading eyes and half-whispered, "Would you send me the answers telepathically while I am taking the test?"

"Sure," I replied, "but before the test make sure you know all of the material in this book." As I said this, I threw down on the table an enormous volume that easily weighed ten kilos. It was one meter long, half a meter wide, half a meter thick, and had extremely small printing on flyleaf pages, of which there were thousands.

"But, but why," she stammered, "Why do I have to do that if you're going to send me the answers telepathically?"

"So that you'll recognize the answers when I send them," I replied.

Comments: This experience presented a very interesting concept: that a knowledge of what one is being guided on is essential to being guided correctly. For instance, how could the Holy Spirit counsel a doctor that the patient he is seeing has appendicitis, if the doctor does not know what an appendix is. If the doctor is familiar with that possibility, it is easy for his Higher Self to send him the correct diagnosis.

So it is with the Spiritual life: one needs to know the principles by which the Holy Power of God operates, so that the Higher Self, as an extension of God and the Holy Spirit, can properly guide one into selecting the right action for a particular situation. "Yes" today, may be "no" tomorrow, and some of these actions, and the principles that govern them, are not what they teach in Sunday school.

Like the young girl in the dream, representing my human self, I was being asked to study the Spiritual principles that govern life, so as to be ready to understand and recognize the Holy Spirit's guidance. Timothy has similar advice in the Christian Bible: "Study to show thyself approved unto God, a workman that needeth not to be ashamed, rightly dividing the word of truth." This may or may not involve book study, as contemplation of one's experiences may be all that is needed. Generally, however, one uses every tool at their disposal.

There is a second major reason for learning the letter of truth; at times, one is left totally without guidance, and is forced to rely on their own wisdom pool of experience and accumulated knowledge in order to make a decision, or choose an action. Of course one will make mistakes doing this but not to worry; a "disturbance in the Force" will definitely register, and the erroneous direction can easily be rectified, leaving one just a bit wiser. Following one's "feel" is a win/win practice: if correct, one did the right thing; if not correct, one now knows what the correct thing is.

One is Soul

THIS INNER HAPPENING was not a dream but more of a mystical, out-of-body experience. After falling asleep one night, I had the awareness of being outside the body for a few brief moments. This was incredible, amazing, an overwhelming epiphany! I did not feel one bit different then when awake in the body! It was unbelievable and I laughed with glee. I was me, Mark, in every way, just like on Earth! I shook my head in disbelief. I was ecstatic. I could not get over it. There was no difference! I felt exactly the same as when in the body.

Comments: This experience, which seemed to take about twenty seconds of Earth time, was a tremendous eyeopener; it so clearly demonstrated that I was Soul, and not the mind/ego. Before this experience, I had thought of Soul as something different from me, removed, unapproachable, far-off, but now, Holy Moly, I was It! I could understand why many Souls were confused immediately after death, asking others if they had died. They hadn't noticed a change.

There is a very thin line between the mind and Soul in the human body. Most people can separate their mind from their emotions, but are unable to distinguish between Soul and mind: in fact, most believe they are their mind and ego, and when they use the pronoun "I" to refer to themselves, they think that it is "them" speaking. Usually it is not. It is their mind/ego.

Their true identity as Soul is just inside that computer, and It is a totally separate consciousness. One, as Soul, cannot be a mind, but one can think they are the mind. How to distinguish between the two? In the human body, it is mainly by feeling. One's very feeling of themselves, their core identity, is Soul: one's feeling of who one is, what one knows, what one does not know, and one's sense of humor. These subjective essences are Soul and are there even when the mind is perfectly still. One way to increasingly discern what is Soul and what is not, is to follow one's intuitive flashes. Not thoughts, but hunches, flashes, premonitions, and prescient feelings: if they prove true, or false, one has gained awareness as to what is Soul's voice, and what is not.

One time I cut myself and needed a band aid. As ridiculous as it sounds, I received a flash that there was one in the freezer. There was, and I had no clue as to how it had gotten there, but the incident helped identify Soul's voice.

Women have a real advantage when it comes to recognizing direction from Soul as they are much more intuitive than men. Generally, men think too much, and must still their mind to hear Soul.

Detachment

THIS BRIEF SNIPPET of a dream had me talking to someone that had a presence but no form. It said, "Mark, you didn't actually take something seriously down there (referring to Earth) did you?"

I blushed copiously and looked down at my feet, "Ah, well, ah yes," I stammered, "guess I did." I'd been totally exposed. Not only had I taken something seriously earlier that day, I had totally lost it in a major meltdown.

Comments: There is an old Chinese saying that says: "As much as you stick out your head into something, that's how much will be chopped off." Rumi states that just when one thinks the payoff is coming, the gain turns into pain. Jesus says not "to make yourselves cozy in this world, it is not your home." Muhammad states: "Be in the world like a traveler or like a passerby and reckon yourself as of the dead." Buddha said: "The good renounce everything."

It would seem the Spiritual giants are in agreement: if one is attached to this world, one will not be successful Spiritually. In addition, do not let the rough and tumble of events on Earth bother one. There are so many truisms in the vernacular that illustrate this truth: chill out; lighten up; forget about it; get a hold of yourself; who cares; relax; move on; deal with it; big deal; so what; cool down; get a grip. These aphorisms, and others similar are good advice for any person, but especially for those totally committed to the Spiritual path, for before they gain everything, they are going to lose it all. If one, at the beginning of their Spiritual journey, could stop caring about the things of Earth, they would save themselves immense pain and misery.

A way to accomplish this, is to become enamored of Spiritual things, and the old cares and Earthly desires will progressively drop away, often without notice.

All is Perfect

ABOUT THIS TIME I had three separate experiences with a teacher in the dream state, although they seemed like real life on the "other side." In the first experience, the teacher took me to different dimensions or planes, and pointed out that they were totally perfect. Perfection was easy to see in the high worlds, one expected it, but the lower dual planes, some lower than Earth, were also excruciatingly perfect.

The forces were represented by linear energy currents flowing at opposite and right angles to each other. The way in which they appeared to be perfect was in how the energies and forces perfectly balanced each other. The currents in the lower worlds seemed either to cancel one another, balance one another, or literally become one another, the negative turning into the positive and vice versa. Everything ran like a very finely tuned machine, or a perfectly spinning top. It was sublime beyond words!

Of course I was stunned: absolutely speechless. One saw to the depths of their being that it was absolutely, painstakingly, perfect! But the topper was yet to come. After visiting many planes of existence, very little of which I brought back to my human consciousness on Earth, the teacher turned to me and said, "Not only are all individual planes perfect in themselves, they inter-relate with each other perfectly as well."

This was too much to absorb; I was dumbfounded! It seemed impossible that those high, high, positive God-Worlds would or could inter-relate with the low dual worlds, many of which were virtual hells. It seemed totally implausible: mind-boggling. Nothing was allowed to be out of balance between the dual forces, or between the dual worlds and the positive God-Worlds; all was in perfect order and balance.

Comments: It is difficult to understand how Creation can be perfect unless one understands a little of the Creator's purpose, especially in the lower dual heavens. It is not to create a paradise where all is goodness and light, but instead create an environment in which Souls can learn and experience the effects of both the positive and negative. This in effect, is eating from the "Tree of the Knowledge of Good and Evil," and eventually becoming a realized Soul. The idea is not for the first plane of Creation to evolve and gradually become the second plane, the idea is for Soul to evolve and eventually be promoted to the second plane of heaven. No need to make the first grade the second grade: its function is to be the first grade.

While life on these lower worlds can look quite violent, and is, no Soul has ever been maimed or killed. Robinson Jeffers, in his instructive poem, "The Bloody Sire," postulates how it is violence that "is the sire of all the world's values." Souls learn the evils of war by going to war.

So it is with truth: it must be learned from experience, and that is exactly what the lower planes of existence provide. It is patently clear that Soul is the Creator's main concern, and is the true "experiencer" of life; although this may be shocking to human sentiments, bodies and personalities seem to mean very little in the grand scheme of life.

Can one imagine what kind of God it would be if IT were not perfect? There would be no continuity of Creation, a prime reason Albert Einstein gave for believing in a Creator.

Once the pilgrim Soul has absorbed the realizations about the nature of good and evil in the lower heavens, they are ready to reenter the "Garden of Eden" (upper positive heavens) and eat from "The Tree of Life." A quatrain from Alexander Pope's "Essay on Man" encapsulates God's perfection succinctly:

Mark K. Olsen

"All nature is art, unknown to thee,
All chance, direction, which thou canst not see;
All discord, harmony not understood;
All partial evil, universal good."

Alexander Pope

The Sport of Souls

THE SECOND EXPERIENCE with this teacher involved the process of creating. First, he demonstrated how something was created in the higher God-Worlds, by instantly manifesting a television set. It was instantaneous; all parts of the set were suddenly there. Then he did exactly the same thing using the energies of the lower dual worlds, and at first, it appeared identical to the first demonstration. However, the teacher asked me to look more closely as he did it again. When I really focused the second time, I could see how the television set came together in successive stages, albeit really fast.

Comments: One of the privileges of Souls in the God-Worlds is the power and freedom to create whatever they desire. One might suggest that Souls' sojourn in the lower worlds is primarily to learn how to create correctly. It is practice time in the lower heavens and the process is quite reversed from the higher heavens. Everything in the lower dual worlds has already been created and exists in a state of flux, so to "create" something, Souls attract already-created events and objects to themselves, or, rearrange lower world forces to simulate true creation as in the higher heavens.

One of the advantages this presents Soul is that in learning to create, think, feel, and imagine correctly, positive already-created states of consciousness and attributes can be attracted to one; these high states are one's future and they are there for the taking: now! This simulated creation in the lower heavens prepares Soul for living and creating "live wire" in the God-Worlds, where the slightest wish, thought, or feeling instantly manifests. Those Souls lacking the self-control needed to establish themselves in these high worlds fall out of them like a rock. Fortunately, this happens rarely, as Souls are rigorously prepared for any advancement over much "real time" and experience; and, there is absolutely no hurry. Eternities go by like June Summer days, and any movement into a higher dimension, is preceded by a long transition period.

In God's Image

THE THIRD AND last experience I had with this teacher took place inside my body. What I was shown was so staggering to the human consciousness that I am seriously hesitant to describe it lest readers think this author insane. Inside myself, we traveled through countless universes, dimensions, planes, and systems I cannot label, and they were the same relative size as the universes that Earth is a part of. The myriads of galaxies, pulsars, suns, and planets were populated with all manner of creatures, including people.

The God-Power streaming through me separated into multiple streams just below the neutral zone, which separated the lower negative dual worlds from the purely positive God-Planes more deeply within. Vast hordes of elemental beings occupied the Astral and Mental worlds, and there were uncountable numbers of angels of every degree, tending to various jobs throughout my universes. The reality of it was staggering!

The teacher explained that as Soul evolved, It would work on mastering the plane within Its own universes corresponding to Its level of growth, while concurrently exploring the corresponding plane of heaven in the "outer" or external universe.

Before I could absorb the least of this, the teacher gave me an image of the planes within my body; there were millions, stretching as far as the eye could see. I was dumbstruck at the thought that eventually, as I grew and evolved throughout eternity, I would have to explore each one of those planes, and its parent plane that it was a microcosm of.

In the consciousness I was in at that moment, which as Soul is ultra-capable, I could not fathom the time involved in simply exploring just one of the planes shown. As I was attempting to retrieve my mental composure, the teacher looked at me and said, "What's the rush?"

Comments: A cardinal principle of esoteric doctrine, no matter the school since they all agree, is that the human being is a microcosm of the macrocosm. Several decades ago, at a prestigious university in Los Angeles, California, lab scientists grew an entire carrot from one cell that had been extracted from a "donor" carrot. The same relationship exists between man, which is one cell of God's Body, and the Body of God.

Within man and woman is an entire Spiritual hierarchy that exactly reflects the hierarchy that runs the entire creation of the Absolute. Man's journey to God is within himself, and while he does simultaneously explore the "outer" universes while projecting in out-of-body consciousness, he is progressively meeting and merging with his very own hierarchy of beings within himself. Eventually, after meeting and blending with each ruler of the various levels within oneself, including the Astral Worlds, the lower Mental Worlds, the Causal Plane, the Higher Mental World, the Unconscious Plane, the Soul Plane, the Worlds of Spirit, the Sound and Light Planes, one meets face to face with the Divine Self at the very center of one's own being. Realizing one's God-Self within is the only possible way to achieve God- Realization, as realizing the Absolute that created this wonder is beyond absurd and always will be.

As to the teacher's parting rhetorical question, it went right to the nexus of a major problem for God-seekers: impatience. When one gets a glimpse of what lays ahead, one is forced to relax and live the now; what does lay ahead that forces one to relax? In one word, eternity. When one sees the scope and breadth of eternity, the idea of striving for future goals looks futile. Ironically, the relaxed seeker unfolds much more quickly than the one actively seeking.

Crazy Love

IF THERE IS one signature quality that the successful Spiritual journey revolves around, it is love. This dream had me placed in a restaurant at the end of a long day. I was the owner of this restaurant, and I was just sitting down to relax after completing the last details of closing for the evening. The chairs were upside down on the tables, the floors had been cleaned, the dishes and cooking utensils had all been washed and shelved, and the lights had been turned low.

As I sat down with a sigh to relax, suddenly there was a commotion on the other side of the room, and a disturbed-looking man burst through the main door, a door that was supposed to have been locked at closing time. The man, who had a rather blank look on his face, gazed vacantly around the room; it was immediately clear that the gentleman did not possess a fully sane mind.

"For crying out loud," I said to myself under my breath, "I'm in no mood for this now." As I glanced over at the man, a small white cloud of ethereal substance detached itself from the man and floated across the room to me: it was his Spirit, of which the man was totally unaware.

"Mark, Mark, we want you to meet this guy," the man's Spirit gushed so excitedly that it was like a new mother showing off her recently born baby to a friend. "Mark, we just love this guy, Mark, just look at these! It's amazingly fantastic, Mark, you won't believe how far he has come! Just look at these, you won't believe it!" As the man's Spirit burst this out, It flashed a series of facsimiles into view that looked somewhat like playing cards, containing events in Its Soul's evolution over the last few billion lifetimes. The man's

Essence simply beamed as It chronicled advances Its Soul had made. Effusively, like a doting parent, it gushed on.

"Mark, we are so proud of this guy, we just love him! We can't wait for you to meet him." It appeared as though the man's Spirit could not contain Itself. Its love for this man was so intense, so all consuming, so white-hot, that I immediately felt ashamed of my initial reaction. I mentally kicked myself and quickly shifted gears.

"Oh of course," I quickly said with a broad smile, "I'd love to meet this guy. Please, please, bring him over right now, I wanna meet him. I can't wait to meet him."

Comments: When I had this dream, I thought I understood its message and I was ashamed of my impatience in dealing with others who were "beginners," as Walt Whitman called them in his wonderful poem of the same name. I vowed to show more sympathy, and more understanding and empathy. Of course this interpretation had merit, but I had missed the central point of the experience, and it was several years before it hit me like a thunderclap one evening as I was contemplating. I was the mentally challenged man, and my Spirit was telling me how much It loved me.

Interrupted Discussion

IN THIS DREAM I was having a discussion with two faculty members at a large university, and it seemed as though it was somewhere in the Causal Plane, or what is generally classified as the top of the third plane of heaven. It was after a class in the evening, and globular lights in strategic places punctuated the darkness. I said to the two professors, "Pardon me, gentlemen, I have an incarnation on the planet Earth that I must attend to."

I then proceeded to incarnate and live a lifetime for sixty years on Earth before translating, and then subsequently rejoined the conversation with the two professors, twelve minutes of their time after I had left for the sixty-year incarnation on Earth.

The two men, who were still standing under one of the lights conversing, smiled at me and one of them asked, "Well, how was it? How did it go?"

I inwardly winced as I quickly replayed the lifetime in my mind, "It got to me, I hate to admit it, but there were times I completely lost perspective."

Comments: Time is such an elastic and relative quality that appears to "stretch out" as one goes into the heavenly planes within. Lifetimes increase geometrically in length, from decades on the Physical Plane to thousands of years on the Astral, and millions and billions of our years on the Causal Plane, to trillions on the fourth plane of heaven. Dissolution of these dual planes also occurs in similar fashion, the time between fresh starts increasing into unimaginably long durations as one moves from the lowest planes of heaven to the top of the fourth plane where this process ends. "…the heavens are the works of Your hands. They will perish…You will roll them up, and they will be changed and replaced by others." (Hebrews 1:10-12) Lifetimes on the Physical Plane, from the perspective of one's Higher Self, are probably a matter of our seconds; however, perhaps the salient point about time, no matter the pace, is that it is always now.

Where I'm From

I REMEMBER HAVING THIS conversation with a gentleman just before awaking one morning. We were on a plane above Earth comparing notes about life on our respective home planets. He complained and whined about the despicable behavior he was forced to witness daily, and was ashamed of the planet he was from, claiming it was the lowest of the low. "Why, just recently," he sneered, "an official had been caught exaggerating public funds! Can you imagine"! If this was the worst that this man could come up with, I thought, it wasn't difficult to see that this gentleman had no idea.

"That's nothing," I said, "Where I'm from there are people who don't even believe there's a God. They call them atheists."

His mouth dropped open, his eyes bulged out, and with a horrified look on his face he gasped, "No, no way." He looked sick.

Comments: The Creation is like a polarized ovoid, being extremely positive at the top, extremely negative at the bottom, and neutral in the center. Earth is very near the negative pole, and is often lumped in with a series of "hells." Life is very short, and the inhabitants of Earth are subjected to every misery possible, even "simulated death." It is strange how this hell is a heaven for some, and they would stay here forever if possible. For those who are more aware, it is truly a hell, and they sacrifice all to graduate out of it.

For the atheists, things are just too big for their twenty/ twenty vision; however, I wouldn't blame an ant for not believing in man, and life, the true religion, teaches the atheists lessons whether they believe in a Creator or not.

Consciousness

ONE NIGHT I had a long dream with the desk next to my bed. It was a large desk, wide and deep, with three drawers to the side of a surface work area, and had been used in an office that planned the construction of freeways in Southern California. My father-in-law worked for the state in such a capacity and I had received the desk from him.

In the dream, the desk conversed with me much as a person would do: it seemed intelligent, and remembered the people and their projects that had worked on its surface. The desk discussed all manner of freeway building, and seemed to personally know other office personnel that had surrounded and worked on it; this included their names and some of their personal idiosyncrasies.

The desk told me its history, including details of its creation by San Quentin Prison inmates in 1948. It was one of those dreams that seemed to go on all night, although it could have been seconds considering the amount my memory brought back. Shortly before I awoke, the desk said to me, "When you get up this morning, pull the top drawer all the way out of the desk and look at the inside-back of the desk. There you will see a tag confirming my birth date and creators."

I awoke clearly remembering the dream and didn't even wait to get dressed. I pulled out the top drawer, which was close to one meter long. I got a flashlight and shined it inside the space created by the vacant drawer. Attached at the back was a yellowed tag about postcard size that read: "Made by prisoners at San Quentin Prison: 1948."

Comments: The fact that all life is conscious is not a new idea, and quite logical to the esoteric thinker. Atoms are obviously part of the Holy Power of God; how could they not be conscious. Admittedly, the consciousness in objects one considers inanimate is very low, but there nonetheless. This is more readily seen in the Plant Kingdom, and is marked in the Animal Kingdom. Many are realizing that the planet itself is conscious, and it helps to understand that one is defining the essence of objects, their Soul if you will, and not the object itself. This is true for the ant, the apple tree, and the archangel.

For instance, the atoms of a desk would have a consciousness so minute that it would be difficult to detect. But put the trillions of atoms together that make up the desk and one has created a combined nexus of consciousness, an entity that is experiencing life at its level in the Mineral Kingdom. And if a desk intrinsically has that much consciousness, how much more consciousness does a car have, a computer, a plant, an animal, a domesticated pet, or a Human Soul. Many Spiritual giants have concluded that not only is all of Creation conscious, it is consciousness itself, at myriads of levels.

This dream provided a sense of perspective regarding the levels of consciousness in all things, and helped develop empathy for all forms of life, whether it is the ballpoint pen that just ran out of ink, the house that's depressed because no one is living there, or the neighbor who just lost a son. Perhaps the golden rule should apply to all life, and not just people. "Do unto everything, as you would have everything do unto you."

The development of consciousness is a prime reason for the Creation, to not only provide a home to evolving Souls, but also to provide the experiences they need to evolve. At the top of Creation, but still below the "Heart of God," there is a vast ocean of Souls, and for general explanatory purposes, they are of two kinds, those that are fully realized, and those that are not.

Innocent and unrealized Souls at the top of Creation descend "Jacob's ladder," step by step, all the way to the lowest level on the physical plane, the Mineral Kingdom, and ascend, step by step, plane by plane, all the way back to the top of Creation fully realized, and prepared to choose a way in which they would like to serve in God's vast Creation. Giving an unrealized Soul a mission in God's vast universes would be like giving a child a position of responsibility.

To complete this journey is not a matter of time, but of experience, and how quickly Soul learns from Its experience. The time involved could not be measured; there are eternities involved and one must realize that it is a forever process without an end. It is so daunting that it makes it imperative to learn how to live the now.

The esoteric definition of consciousness refers to the consciousness of Soul, not the consciousness of the human mind, and that includes everything Soul has learned in Its evolutionary growth forever; Soul's memory of all that It has learned and experienced is Its understanding.

Knowledge when applied through experience leads to realization; realizations become wisdom; wisdom becomes consciousness. Consciousness and wisdom cannot be transferred from one Soul to another; if consciousness and realization could be transferred, obviously God would have simply given it to Soul. No saint or master can take one to live in heaven; they may take a Soul to visit and learn, but the right to establish oneself on any plane has to be earned, whether it is the lowest plane or the highest. Soul's vibration rate must match the dimension It wishes to live in, and it is not possible to fake a high state of consciousness.

I Have to Leave

THIS EXPERIENCE OCCURRED during one night when I was half in and half out of waking consciousness. I had a large orange ringtail cat named Govinda who had turned into a big softie, and he loved to sleep on my chest when I was lying down. For this reason, I kept my bedroom door closed at night lest Govinda come in and disturb my sleep.

One night as I lay asleep, I felt him jump up on the bed, even though there was no way he could be in the room. He was a heavy cat and I could feel his individual steps depress the bed as he walked up to my face, even though he was in his Astral Body. He looked at me and simply messaged, "I have to leave."

The next morning I awoke with a clear memory of the night before, but I rather desperately hoped it wasn't true. With trepidation I opened the bedroom door and prayed Govinda would be there to greet me, but he wasn't, and I never saw him again or learned anything of his disappearance.

Comments: Losing a beloved pet is often a difficult experience, but in this case it was modified somewhat by his farewell. I didn't have to worry about trying to find him. It also verified what I had learned up to this point: that the animals are Souls just like humans and other entities. Many of the more evolved animals have extensive missions: it may involve protecting the humans that they are interacting with, teaching and helping other animals, or contributing to mankind in other ways, even to the sacrificing of their physical bodies for work or food.

Souls that are in the bodies of domesticated pets, like horses, cats and dogs, are processing the transition from group Souls to individuation, and will over much time enter into human bodies.

They are mankind's children following in their footsteps. No pet owner questions an animal's ability to love, a sure testimonial to their evolved consciousness, and many people love their pets more than any human being they care to know, and are loved more in return than any other human being cares to do.

Animals and birds that are not inter-relating with man belong to group souls, and upon leaving their body, rejoin the group Soul of which they are a member, transmitting the benefits of their experience to the entire group. Even science on this level has discovered this principle concerning the evolutionary growth of consciousness. Imagine the process between Souls.

Ecstasy

IN THIS SHORT dream experience, I was drifting through the sky on some upper plane of heaven, sitting back as though in a lounge chair. I was so happy I could barely maintain my equilibrium.

I thought to myself, what just happened to make me so ecstatic, I cannot believe how good I feel. I have never felt happiness like this!

As I was thus engaged attempting to trace the reason for my joy, I saw another Soul drifting towards me. "Hi!" I gushed out, so loud that it would normally be embarrassing. "Hello!" I shouted again with a big smile, totally unable to restrain myself as though he were a long lost brother that I had been searching for. I loved the man instantly. "Howdy friend!" I shouted again uncontrollably.

"Hiiiiii!" he shouted back, with such happy abandon that I couldn't help but notice that he was overjoyed as well! He laughed and waved and shouted out way too loud, "Hello! how are you! what a pleasure to see you!" He was giggling as he drifted by; I had never seen a happier man.

It then hit me: everyone here is happy; they don't even need a reason. It is just the way it is here, the Souls here are always this happy.

Comments: Many people, when they visualize or imagine some beautiful plane of heaven, picture themselves enjoying the environment, but in the same consciousness as they have here on Earth. Such is not the case. One's consciousness and awareness expands commensurate to the distance one goes within, and one understands and knows everything concerning the planes below them. One's measure of joy, freedom, wisdom, power, awareness, and love all increase exponentially to astounding levels that are difficult to conceive of.

Once Soul enters the first positive plane above the dual worlds, there is no pain, suffering, negativity, unhappiness, dirt, dust, or mortality. Souls are so overwhelmingly happy that there is little incentive to move on, and while Souls there have a mission they have chosen, they do it in the most relaxed, contented way. Ecstasy is the norm.

Be You

THIS WAKING EXPERIENCE happened on a beautiful spring day in Glen Ellen, California, a little town in wine country, seventy kilometers above San Francisco. I had just arrived home from seeing a movie that I found blasphemous, and I decided to take a walk down Madrone Avenue towards the Sonoma River and contemplate my reaction to the movie.

The movie, which clearly had an ax to grind, savagely parodied the Savior of the Christian religion, and the hate was so palpable that the excuse that this was humor or satire was as thin as an atom of air. I am sure the movie's creators thought it hilarious, along with their sympathizers and those who love to mock other people's beliefs.

As I walked towards the river, I argued with myself as to whether I was justified in feeling repulsed by the movie, or if I was overreacting to raw humor. After all, I reasoned, I am not a Christian and have sarcastically roasted society's icons more than most critics have. What's the harm in a little fun, and I never have respected sacred cows.

However, a deeper part of me did not agree, and felt that there were limits, and wasn't so sure that mocking God, or those who their worshippers thought was God, was a good idea.

But what about detachment Mark, the opposing side countered, you're going to let a little movie fun upset you. Get a grip. It's just a movie.

This inner argument, back and forth, went on and on as I approached the river, which flowed some fifteen meters below the highway, and I started angling down a stairway-like embankment on the side of the road towards the river below.

I was nearly to the riverbank when suddenly there was a tremendously loud explosion. BLAM! I froze in shock. I had no idea what had happened but it became immediately apparent. A bottle thrown from a passing car above had hit my left knee with a tremendous report, shattering the bottle into a thousand pieces. I stood there completely stunned. The barrel of the bottle had somehow hit my knee so perfectly that I did not feel a whit of pain, and the collision had virtually vaporized the bottle. I looked up towards the highway above me but the car from which the bottle had been tossed was already long gone, and the fact that the thrown bottle had hit me was obviously unintentional as I had been completely out of the car's field of vision.

I looked down at my feet. The bottle had completely shattered into hundreds of tiny chips no bigger than a raisin, and there was only one small piece of the label from the bottle that I could see, held together by four small bits of glass glued to the backside of it. I picked it up. It read, *Bu*, it was from a *Budweiser* beer bottle.

Comments: This experience, to use a common idiom, was a real mindblower, and it primarily helped my understanding in two areas, the first being to further identify and legitimize my own basic "inner feel." I felt as though the Higher Self was condoning the right to be repulsed by the movie, not as a matter of right or wrong, but to the point that the reaction was just naturally "me." The advice to "be yourself" is ubiquitous in self-help literature, but to follow that truism requires knowing your Self, which knowledge seems to be hidden sometimes among the mass of inner components competing for attention at one's own personal council table within.

The second thing that really got my attention was the total control of events that the Holy Spirit, or Higher Self, manifested in engineering this experience: there were so many variables that needed to mesh in order for it to happen: the buying of the correct beer; the fact that the drinker had finished drinking it before arriving at the bridge; the drinker's urge to throw the bottle; the timing, strength, and angle of the toss; the speed of the car; the position and pace of my walking; the positioning of the bottle in mid-air as to hit my knee precisely right in mid-stride; the shattering of the bottle into incredibly small pieces, leaving only a perfectly extrapolated piece of the label with two letters showing; the fact that there was absolutely no pain; in addition, there were many other variables impossible for me to know. In such incidents, there is a plethora of miracles.

Robert Frost wrote a beautiful poem entitled "Design," in which he questions to what level of life God's control or "design" applies. Does God control everything or is it compromised by free will? He rhetorically asks whether the killing of a white moth by a waiting spider is by design, or chance. It is a good question and I do not know the answer; however, in this experience, the level of design went to incredible lengths, and it seemed as if there were no detail that the Higher Self did not control to the last atom.

Of course this control applies to all life, whether one is driving on a crowded freeway, or is contemplating in an easy chair.

All In

ONE BEAUTIFUL DAY in Southern California I traveled to Big Dalton Canyon and picked a pastoral location for a "session" next to a rushing stream. The spot I was sitting in overlooked a moderately sized waterfall with a spillway to the near side, and the sounds of the swirling waters sprinting to lower levels were soothing comfort.

Presently I noticed a California newt crawling towards the spillway from some ten meters away. The newt is a cute little salamander with smooth human-like skin and bulging eyes that are way too big for its little smiling "E.T." face. These adorable little amphibians swim and breed in the water, and on land they walk extremely slowly, looking as though each tiny little step has been contemplated for several seconds.

It looked as though it would be twenty minutes before navigating the ten meters to the edge of the stream, and when arriving, he would discover a choice: because of a low wall along the near side of the spillway, there was only one little spot where dirt had accumulated, forming a little ramp for the newt to access the top of the wall, where if he chose, he could jump into the raging torrent of water gaining the pond three meters below.

Or, if that looked too dangerous, he could walk for another twenty meters downstream where there was access to the pond. As he trudged step by little step, I became increasingly interested in what choice he would make. To jump into the spillway looked like suicide for the fragile little guy, as the swollen stream was full and fast. Conversely, if he decided to walk downstream it would be a lot of walking.

Finally, he arrived at the ramp and gingerly climbed to the top of the wall, seeing the spillway of rushing water in front of him for the first time. He looked at it for a full minute, and then gazed downstream as if gauging the time it would take him to walk down to the next possible entry spot in the stream.

Another two minutes went by: the tension increased as I waited for his decision. Suddenly, with all four legs and tail stretched out, he sprang backward off the wall into the spillway with a tremendous leap and was immediately lost to sight.

Comments: This nature play struck me as a wonderful example of commitment, as though the newt had total faith in his God; this is exactly the faith needed to be successful Spiritually.

It is true that all Spiritual effort is rewarded, and that every sincere appeal to God is answered. However, to have Spiritual experiences, and not just a warm temporary feeling, one must be "all in." For those pure Souls who are unfamiliar with the card game of poker, "all in" is a term used to describe placing all of your chips (money) on one's bet. It is all or nothing. When that newt jumped backwards into the spillway's rushing waters, he exhibited the attitude needed to be successful Spiritually, and he reminded me of Milarepa, the great Tibetan Master who dove into the River of God the same way.

Many people want God in their life, but they also want their desires at the same time. *In the Gospel of St. Thomas,* The Christ within Jesus says: "No man can ride two horses." He also advises against trying to serve "two masters," and through parables suggests that God be one's "pearl of great price," the "big fish" that is kept, the treasure of one's heart, the choice of God over mammon.

Even with total commitment, it is indisputable that man cannot do this alone. Of course every person tries this but the mind will not give up its cherished desires, and asking it to is similar to asking the fox to guard the chicken coop. Tell a woman or man to become detached about their children, or a rich person to part with goods, or a person in power to step down: no way. If that is true, how does one go about trying to develop Spiritually?

It is very simple. If one does their devotions every day and asks God, or one's Higher Self, to do their will with them, the Holy Spirit will gradually and lovingly surrender the seeker step by step, something the seeker could never do alone. Old habits and desires will progressively be replaced by new directions, and the process will be so gradual and voluntary that it often seems as though one gave up nothing at all: at least nothing of value.

One out of a thousand seekers is "all in"; the rest, in spite of what they proclaim, are testing the waters with their big toe, gradually gaining the courage to dive in all the way and swim for their Salvation.

The Magic Ingredient

ONE DAY WHILE driving around wine country north of San Francisco, I picked up a student hitchhiker who was on his way to Sonoma State University. He was a young man in his mid-twenties from Germany, and after settling the details of where he was going, I asked him directly to tell me about his life. He accepted readily.

He said that he had studied at various universities all over the world: Oxford, the Sorbonne, Yale, Beijing University, and several others I'd never heard of. He spoke four languages fluently, and shared that his main studies had involved world religions. In fact, he stated with no loss of pride, he had wanted to learn classical *Sanskrit* while in India which would have enabled him to read the *Vedas* in their original manuscripts.

He had three PhD's and five Masters of Arts, which of course included the pre-requisite four-year degrees. Since I had done a little reading in the religious fields, I asked him to share what religious literature he had studied. He readily responded and it was very impressive.

Since India was fresh on his mind, he began with their literature: he had read the *Mahabharata* of course, (the longest epic poem in the world) of which the *Bhagavad-Gita* is a tiny part; the *Ramayana* (another wonderfully long epic); nearly all of the almost two hundred *Upanishads,* the four Vedas; all eight volumes of the *Granth Sahib,* by Gopal Singh, which is the Scriptural Guru of the Sikh religion; Johnson's translation of the *Buddhacarita,* (Acts of the Buddha); the *Yoga Shastra* of *Hemchandrachaya,* and several Buddhist *Sastras* I'd never heard of.

He said he loved the Sant Mat teachings of Northern India, and that their beliefs on the Light and Sound were the highest teachings he had found. He continued with Plato's works claiming *The Phaedo* was his favorite, as the logic Socrates used to prove Soul's immortality really appealed to him.

He had devoured the main authors of Theosophy and said a good shortcut was to read A.E. Powell because he had extrapolated the best of Blavatsky, Leadbeater, and Besant. Of course he had read the *Koran* but liked the Islamic mystics Hafiz, Jami, Navoi and Rumi the best. He had studied the *Bible* extensively, and claimed that Gnosticism should have triumphed in the early days of Christianity, because after all, they had the deeper truth. He loved the Tao and his favorite American writer was Paul Twitchell.

He continued as I grew preoccupied with my own thoughts. There was no doubt the gentleman was a genius, and I felt some kinship with him regarding his search for truth, but there was something obviously missing. He then proceeded to drop a bombshell on me that completely confirmed my suspicions.

"None of them work," he said.

"What do you mean?" I asked.

"None of the religions and paths that I've studied work," he repeated. "I've tried them all. They just don't work." He said this with complete conviction as though the possibility he could be wrong did not exist. This declaration amused me and I felt as though my Higher Self was nudging me to reply to this outrageous assertion.

"There is a magic ingredient," I interjected, "a magic ingredient that if applied, any of the paths you studied would have worked." We were within a kilometer of his destination, and I was not going to say anything more unless he asked.

It was apparent he did not want to ask, and he stayed silent for a minute as we approached his building. There was a palpable tension in the car as he struggled with himself, internally debating whether he should give me the satisfaction of telling him, of all people, what the magic ingredient was. I pulled up to the curb.

Finally, with a sneer on his face, and in a tone dripping with sarcastic condescension, he asked, "Okay, what do YOU think is the magic ingredient?"

I looked him straight in the eye and said in a strong voice, "Sincerity!"

He gasped and his eyes widened with a look of guilt. He was stunned! He knew he was not sincere, and he knew that I knew he was not sincere. He turned his face away and quickly left the car without a word.

Comments: The Christ within Jesus said that the "pure in heart would see God": perhaps purity of heart is the equivalent of sincerity. It is the only ingredient needed in the Spiritual life and leads to all the other "fruits of the Spirit," be one an ant or an Archangel.

It does not matter how many books you have read; many God-Realized Souls were illiterate. The old adage is true: the mind is a great servant but a poor master. It is hilarious that the ego of man thinks its mind intelligent when in fact he suffers from total ignorance.

It brings to mind a famous quote that appears in Spiritual literature all over the world, this version being Gurdjieff's: "A person has the chance to be born again; before they can be born again, they must become awake; before they can become awake they must die."

Ironically, most Souls on this planet are building and strengthening their mind's ego lest their personality not survive the "personality death" that awaits them. It is a real execution to find out that one is totally ignorant, powerless, and helpless, but it is a death that leads to everlasting life.

The Judgment

THIS DREAM SEEMED to go on all night, and involved picking up people who had been summoned for judgment, and then escorting them to their trial.

On the way to their judgment, I had long conversations with them and they told me the circumstances that had led to their summons. Some of those charged were very likable, and it seemed to me they would be totally exonerated, and I told them as much. Others were very disagreeable and the things they had been charged with were quite terrible. I was privately sure these latter examples would have the book thrown at them, maybe even be executed.

I was wrong in every single case: those whom I thought guilty were released without even a reprimand, and those likable Souls I thought innocent received the full force of the law. Many of the cases I had thought a no-brainer; I was totally confident in my opinion. Not one time was I right.

Comments: Three of the obstacles to successful judgments, if ever a thing were possible, is that everyone is operating from different levels of consciousness, personal values are relative, and another Soul's karma is a total unknown.

One does not judge a four-year-old child harshly for not understanding physics, nor should one judge a "young" Soul for believing in cannibalism; it is their level and state of consciousness. It is unfair of the more evolved Souls to project their values onto the less evolved, and the difference in their individual understanding could be due to a difference of millions of lifetimes. Pythagoras asked one to treat those "younger" as one's children, those equal as brothers and sisters, and those ahead of one as parents.

As to personal values, relativity reigns supreme. One person's medicine is another's poison; one worshipper's God is another believer's Satan; one person's heaven is another person's hell. How does one judge that? Many have pointed out that due to ignorance and gross stupidity, it is unwise to judge even oneself. One's mental incapacity is virtually total.

One is very fortunate if they understand anything of their own personal karma, let alone anyone else's.

There is an old Tibetan fable that relates how God noticed that Souls were not living righteously, so he appointed one of his Archangels to preside over a court that would render appropriate judgments and punishments. Of course the Archangel appointed to the task took his job very seriously, attempting to be as judicious as possible, giving much time and study to each case and weighing every possible factor.

After attempting to resolve several cases, the Angel was so totally frustrated that he went to see God about being relieved of the responsibility. The Angel felt there were too many variables of differing weight to be taken into consideration, making a fair reckoning nigh impossible. The differences in Souls and their experiences were simply too great to properly account for.

Of course, God understood, and to solve the problem, decided to simply have each Soul receive back Its very own creations, and thus, the law of karma was born.

All is Provided

ONE EVENING I was reading a book by a gentleman from India named Maharaj Sawan Singh Ji, who was reminding his followers that everything needed was already provided by the Holy *Shabd* (Word). As I read this, my thoughts were interrupted by the awareness of a troubling sliver in my finger that I had tried and failed to extract several times. I said aloud to myself, "Well Spirit, I need a tweezers to get this sliver out; where are the tweezers?"

At that moment my roommate came into the room asking if I wanted to play some Frisbee in the dark. We often did this, each of us standing under a streetlight a good distance apart. I agreed and upon exiting the front door stepped on some object on the landing: it was a tweezers, somewhat rusted but totally functional. It was too much to accept, I could not believe it. I yelled," no way!" and threw them over the front house on our lot towards the street.

One minute later, while playing in the darkened street, my roommate threw me a bounce pass, careening it off the pavement, and it came to me at eye level, wobbling erratically. I caught it, and stuck in the top of the Frisbee, with one prong puncturing clean through the plastic, was the tweezers.

Comments: I have shared this experience with others and they usually have similar stories, often bordering on the miraculous. Now, when needing some trivial item, I look around knowing it must be within reach; and, it often is. The important things are always within reach, as there is never a time when the Higher Self's help is not available.

"But rather seek ye the Kingdom of God; and all these things shall be added onto you." This scripture verse, said by the Christ within Jesus, is the experience of those sincerely devoted to God. All of their needs are supplied be they physical, emotional, mental, or Spiritual, and fulfillment becomes a reality.

Ufo or Ifo

THIS ADVENTURE BEGAN on a warm autumn evening at Sugarloaf State Campground near Kenwood, California. My wife and I loved camping, and we had decided to sleep under the stars sans tent. We pitched a tent in the spot reserved, but hiked a kilometer further into the park where we might enjoy more space. There we spread our sleeping bags on the edge of a beautiful meadow and lay down, gazing up at the stars on a crystal-clear night.

At some point in the middle of the night, while sleeping, I became conscious of traveling in a spacecraft, about the size of a gymnasium. It was circular and dome-shaped, and I was relaxing in a moderately sized lounge towards the top of the ship which contained portholes like one might see on an ocean ship.

I glanced out one of the windows and recognized some oak-covered hills that lie just north of San Francisco, which meant that I was close to the campground that contained my sleeping body. I proceeded to descend to the bottom of the ship where a technician had opened a circular hatch in the center-bottom of the craft. The room was full of technical gear and looked like a *Star Wars* movie scene. The crewmember turned on a bright white light that projected a circular beam onto the ground.

I stepped up to the hatch and said to the technician, a beautiful young brown-skinned woman who looked very capable, "Leave the light on for a few seconds; I want my body to see it." I jumped into the light.

The very next thing I was conscious of was waking up in my sleeping bag on the ground. I sat up. There in the middle of the meadow was a circle of neon-like white light, fifteen meters in diameter, and it was capped about one meter off the ground as though it had an invisible lid. There was nothing I could see above it in the sky, and there was not a beam visible traveling to the ground.

I awakened my wife who lay next to me, and she groggily sat up and witnessed the circular disc. Then as though a switch had been flipped, we were in total blackness again. I went back to sleep happy that my wife had witnessed a small part of the experience.

In the morning I inspected the meadow just to reassure my doubtful mind that there was not an ulterior explanation for the light. There was nothing.

Comments: This experience is not unusual, and thousands have similar tales to tell. Of course, it is confusing to people who do not understand that one can leave their physical body, enter their Astral form, and travel in all manner of ways, whether it be flying at incredible speeds, or climbing into a space ship bound for some destination beyond one's Astral capabilities.

The more evolved simply project their consciousness to wherever they choose, often by switching to their own inner component that resides in the dimension that they care to visit. Traveling only occurs in the lower heavens where time and space exist; it is unnecessary in the higher planes, where differing levels of consciousness are what separate the various regions.

This experience helped create a broadened perspective, and I decided to type it up and send it to *Fate Magazine,* which publishes unusual experiences of this kind. They said no thanks. I suspect they thought that the story was made up.

Contact

IT WAS A short time later when I had another experience with a UFO, and as is usual with the Holiest of Powers, It will dwell on a particular subject for a time, and then move on to other aspects of one's personal path: It seldom returns to the previous lesson and expects one to have extrapolated and applied what was needed from their experiences.

In this nighttime event, just before waking up, I had the consciousness of coming back to the body, momentarily preparing to enter at the place on the time track that I was experiencing on Earth. As I returned towards the desired spot, it felt as though I were moving at an incredible speed, gradually slowing as I approached the desired entry point.

To my side, images flashed by of events in the future, much like a movie might show calendar pages flashing by to denote the passing of time. These images were facsimiles of events, much as if one condensed a long movie into one image, with thousands of bits of information. Souls in the lower heavens exchange facsimiles routinely as a preferred method of communication, and absorb all the data from a facsimile at once; in the higher heavens this is not necessary.

As I came to a stop, I looked over at the last picture visible, before the place on the time track I was to enter, where I would be "living" such facsimiles. The image was clear. A spacecraft from Earth that looked much like a *Star Wars* shuttlecraft, was docking with a large alien ship that was about the size of a ten-story building.

Everything about the event was clear immediately. The spacecraft was on its way to a distant destination in another galaxy but was in the "neighborhood" and stopped by to make contact.

It was parked in orbit around one thousand kilometers above the planet, and its occupants had contacted Earth, inviting a group of the planet's seven or eight best to visit their ship. Contact would be handled through glass partitions, sealed to prevent accidental contamination as the aliens wanted no part of Earth's atmosphere. I received the impression that secrets regarding space travel and energy would be shared.

As I gazed at the image, I said to myself, "Now that would be in about forty years."

My next impression was of waking up in the body.

Comments: Let me begin by saying this poor fool has never predicted anything, but if one were to try, predicting contact by aliens would be a safe prediction. It is fair to say that the planet is being prepared for a visitation. The signs are everywhere, especially in the entertainment industry and science.

One only has to think of the *Star Wars* series, or of *Star Trek*, or of countless movies and shows that have dealt with the concept of alien life. It is endemic to modern culture, and the idea that life is probable everywhere in the universe has become increasingly accepted.

There was a newspaper report recently about a party in Manhattan where several revelers out on the balcony witnessed a UFO. One of them ran into the apartment shouting, "They're here, they're here!" People are no longer wondering if aliens are coming, but when.

Science is also moving step by step to the rediscovery of life elsewhere than Earth. There seems to be a hierarchy of discoveries that gradually prepare and acclimate the populace to the possibilities that are just ahead. There is little doubt that many of the most vulnerable on Earth may be seriously unbalanced by the eventual contact with another species. Many will have their religious beliefs compromised, and basic assumptions will be threatened. One positive result will be that the event will unite the feuding peoples of Earth as never before, as they realize that they have more than less in common.

This inner experience happened in 1989, making the dream's prediction 2029, but wisdom dictates that it is nearly impossible to predict a time or event in the lower heavens which shift and change continuously. It is like trying to predict the next image in a kaleidoscope.

If and when Earth resumes contact with other planets and peoples it will not be the first time. This has happened hundreds of times in Earth's long history as civilizations come and go like the seasons.

Nothing Wrong Here

IN THIS DREAM experience, I was cast in the role of an important Spiritual figure that had been invited to tour and inspect a religious community on another planet. The citizens there had carefully prepared a welcoming reception, and a train of dignitaries followed along as I was escorted through their community.

All communication was telepathic and there was a relative silence for so many gathered people. Throngs of onlookers lined the streets as I slowly moved along, and many followed after being passed by the lead group. The people were uniformly dressed in toga-like white robes, and were extremely deferential; they were very proud of their society and wanted everything to appear just perfect.

I played the part of a beneficent leader and nodded approval at various instances to particular people and religious displays. The atmosphere was rather solemn and there was a mild subsurface tension as though the outcome of this inspection held some importance.

Suddenly there was a loud inarticulate shout from a woman to the far side. She was sitting alone in a contorted position on the ground. No one was near the woman and her shout had been so loud that everything had come to a sudden dead halt.

Palpable waves of disapproval instantly soaked the air; the crowd knew this woman and disliked her intensely, and they were becoming incensed at the fact that she was possibly destroying the ceremony, and perhaps the results of the visit as well. She appeared to be a total outcast.

I looked over at the woman with twisted limbs, sitting in an unnatural position, and she sent me a wave picture that contained a strong plea, that if translated into words might say, "Please tell me, am I ok, or am I headed in the wrong direction?"

The crowd stirred uneasily: they thought the woman impertinent and their objections to her filled the air with angry black and red thought forms. This woman used some type of drug to augment her Spiritual life and beliefs, and the people had wanted nothing to do with her for some time. The substance she used had grossly compromised her physical body and crippled her limbs. It was doubtful she could walk.

I studied the woman's aura. It was immediately apparent that she was considerably more evolved than the other residents of this community, with many high states of consciousness readily discernable in her magnetic field. Beautiful pastels of rose, blue and yellow flashed through the translucent cloud of light swirling around her. She had transcended the conventional religious paradigm that dominated this people's belief system. She may be the lead channel for the Holy Spirit in this area, I thought to myself.

I sent out a massive wave of calming benediction, in effect saying, "I see nothing wrong here." I then continued walking on while the procession stood silently stunned.

Tears streamed down the woman's face as a massive burst of joy, comprised of pale-blue light framed with primrose yellow, shot outward from the corona surrounding her head, into the surrounding atmosphere.

Comments: There are many seekers who feel guilty and impure because they are using drink or drugs, and often both. Many times, family or religion is on their back about their habits. Ironically, many of these seekers are using these substances for their Spiritual path, imbibing them to still the mind, or adjust their consciousness to a desired state. Others partake to balance their Spiritual practices.

The question is not necessarily, "Should one use these substances?" Sometimes, for those who indulge, the question is, "What is one's attention on when they are being used?"

For those uninterested in Spirituality, who cares? For those attempting to cooperate with their Higher Self, everything is used to Spiritual advantage.

Hell is full of Souls who never touched a drop of alcohol or took one drug, and heaven has many who did both. That drunk in the gutter may be a God-lover. It is one's state of consciousness that matters, not one's habits, even if the habits have deleterious effects.

Naturally, it is wise to be in balance and have good control of anything used, moderation being ideal. However, if one is struggling on that score, the Holy Spirit will gradually bring the problem under control, provided the person is maintaining daily contact with their Higher Self, and using Its support to cooperate with Its guidance.

As to why a handicapped woman symbolized my human self, two main reasons come to mind, the first being that it gave me a backdoor to escape the fact that it represented me. I could protect my ego and perhaps say to myself, "Thank God I'm not that person." The Holy Power of God is so very kind and gentle, that if one is unready to accept the next step, an alternate interpretation of Spiritual experiences is usually available.

In addition, the girl represented my anima, the feminine psychological consciousnesses of my lower bodies, which although frozen and contorted by my patriarchal upbringing, nonetheless contained the higher truth: this feminine center was intuitively closer to Soul than the dominant masculine consciousness that controlled me at that time.

The Catch

MOST PEOPLE BEGIN a Spiritual path looking to have a better life. Some want truth, some want peace; others want adventure and startling experiences, while many want to heal. The Holy Spirit is more than willing to grant the various requests although some take time; however, there is a catch.

The God-Power, in effect, strikes a deal with the devotee. It in effect says: "Okay, We will progressively grant your Spiritual requests, but We would appreciate that you consider attempting to cooperate with the suggestions We send your way, to the best of your ability."

The Holy Spirit is very polite. If one does not follow the suggestions, melding to them as best as they are able, the growth stops at that point until the person decides to incorporate the direction that has been politely indicated. Those Souls not unfolding or growing are locked at a point of non-cooperation; the Holy Power is willing to wait patiently forever; there is no rush, and Soul's free will is respected.

Recreating the Beautiful

IN THIS INNER experience I was feeling extremely sad and depressed. Some situation of incredible beauty had just taken place, and now it was gone forever.

Just what the event was I do not know, but it was wonderfully incredible and was now history; it pained me greatly to know it would never be again. It was beauty so intense that I had wept to see it.

As I sat in a stupor of self-pity, a voice began speaking to me inside my head, "Mark, Mark, don't be sad, beauty has to be continually recreated. Do it again Mark. Create another beautiful happening. Go ahead Mark. Set it up. Do it."

Comments: Esotericism does not believe in a second cause. This means that one is totally responsible for everything in one's life, as one is the first cause and creator of every single thing about them: not virtually, literally.

Through the imagination, mind, emotions, and actions, one not only creates the events and happenings in their life, karma if you will, but they have also fashioned their very own being by what they imagine themselves to be.

The imagination can be divided into two layers for explanative purposes: there is the conventional imagination that one uses for everyday activities, creative ventures, problem solving, one's next action and the like; there is the deeper core of this creative faculty that is the very spark of one's being, and creates the very way one looks at themselves; "for as he thinketh in his heart, so is he." (Proverbs 23:7)

One is exactly what this deeper layer of the imagination has created, and to change oneself, one must change their imaginative perception of themselves. The easiest and truest way in which to do this is to identify oneself as Soul. Why not? It is true.

The idea that something else is responsible for the events in one's life, such as an evil force or a devil, is devoid of Spiritual logic; there is no evil force opposing God or man, and what evil there is comes from man, not from God or some boogeyman. Spiritual adulthood means taking responsibility for one's own actions, as karma implies.

The Shadow

THOSE WHO MAKE an effort to go "inside" not only encounter their Higher Selves, but their lower selves as well. The shadow, or dark side, is extremely powerful and not to be ignored. The naïve do not believe they have one. Carl Jung, the co-founder of modern psychology and a master of the unconscious, claims that the shadow does not integrate well with the rest of the personality. Yet, to a point it must, or one's Spiritual journey will be compromised.

Many fight their darker center and attempt to repress or suppress it, but that does not work as its power and energy will build cumulatively, eventually exploding out, and often at the worst possible time. A relationship must be established with this component in order to control it. There are several approaches to forming a give and take with the shadow, which plays a large role in one's everyday life.

The first may be to understand it; the shadow is very conscious, and has been maligned and marginalized for uncountable lifetimes. It knows the raw truth and is angry at being ignored, suppressed, preached to, blamed, censored, and cursed. It is hurt and wants to be acknowledged. Nightmares are often the shadow's impulses, which are anxious to manifest and "get out." Who cannot understand hate, anger, jealousy, revenge, and rage? When the shadow grabs the central microphone, one's ego is the shadow; one should know how it feels. Fighting and war are shadow heaven. It helps to know this.

A second approach is to give in to it within defined parameters. For instance, one might occasionally treat it to rich food, a lazy day off work, or telling that annoying person to back off. The darker side has no moral compass, yet knows the unembellished truth, and it becomes extremely frustrated when unable to vent. A solution to this is to let this part of one tell the truth rather directly in appropriate situations, without letting it fully engage in destructive actions. This relieves this component's pressure without disastrous consequences.

For instance, perhaps a young lady's boyfriend did not call as promised, and the girl is extremely upset, ready to go into a rage. Instead of letting her darker side out too far and perhaps ending the relationship, she calmly tells her delinquent friend: "When you didn't call last night as promised, you disrespected me and hurt my feelings, and I am angry."

Of course, there may be a confrontation, but her action appeases her dark side enough to possibly prevent a far worse development that could end badly. Without venting the truth this way, the young lady risks worse the next time as her anger has not been mollified; frequently, nightmares occur as this energy fights for release. Dreams of being chased by something horrifying, running in water, or being paralyzed may occur.

Another helpful technique for venting the dark side is to pick a target that is trivial, and will not land one in big trouble from the one attacked. Perhaps it is a cardboard box. One might tongue lash it, curse it, crush it, beat it, burn it, and then jump up and down on the ashes. No harm done and the box will profit from the infusion of energy.

Physical exercise is also very effective, so is lovemaking, and according to Mark Twain, swearing helps.

The shadow is strong and is ready to defend one, whether it is with a convincing lie, a fight, or flight. It does not care about anyone else and has absolutely no compunction about exhibiting prejudice, participating in violence or killing. It does not change or evolve, and it laughs at all forms of social correctness. It is very brave. It loves lewdness, sex, cursing, and it has a filthy sense of humor.

The dark side is one hundred times more prevalent in everyone than well-meaning people would ever expect. It has both a feminine and masculine side. Joseph Conrad authored two extremely insightful stories concerning this side of man: the first is the novel, *Heart of Darkness*, the second is the short story, "The Secret Sharer." They demonstrate what successfully incorporating the shadow into one's total being can mean for an individual: strength, serenity, truth, bravery, self-confidence. They also demonstrate what happens when the dark side takes over the individual: hate, anger, violence, tyranny, lust, and other siblings of such ilk.

There were many experiences with this side of myself. In several, the dark side, represented by a large bear, attacked, and despite evasive maneuvers, I could never get away or kill the bear for good, despite shooting it time after time. In another instance, a wild-looking caveman burst through the front door and attacked me. Once it was a wild horse, and it chased me down and killed me with a long knife. Another time it manifested as a beautiful young woman dressed in black, who fiercely tried to kill me.

The biggest eyeopener occurred during an experience with my Higher Self, and although unseen, It had somehow made me aware that It would open a small special door, allowing me to see into my dark side. My Higher Self opened the door and then shut it immediately; for one brief second I looked through the door.

I realize that normally the shadow is regarded as a sub-part of the mind, but fellow Souls, when I glanced through that door, I saw that I, as the human consciousness, was totally "dark"; I was all shadow. A longer look at the depths of that darkness would have completely depressed me.

After many years of gaining a tiny bit of understanding about this side of my lower nature, and making somewhat of a deal with it, I, as the human Soul, met it face to face in a dream. It was cute and funny in a strange way, as it was a curious reversal of meeting the Higher Self; I was looking down, instead of up.

The representation of my dark side looked exactly like me, and as I reached out with a smile and shook its hand, it could not face me directly but blushed and avoided eye contact, feeling ashamed and looking down at his feet.

This by no means ended experiences with this aspect of my lower nature, and oftentimes the challenges this side presented were more than I could handle. St. Paul, in the book of *Romans*, chapter seven of the *Christian Bible,* well describes the battle with this master of absolutely terrible impulses, and how one ends up doing "what they would not."

There were dreams of being in runaway vehicles without lights or brakes and a jammed accelerator. There were continuing control issues and many meltdowns. As one unfolds, they process more energy; the shadow is also a recipient of this energy and matches the efforts of the devotee to control it. The saviors and saints that are worshipped by millions had the strongest shadows in the world, and may have needed all of their power to control it. The "give and take" with this element is never over while in the lower bodies.

A comforting thought is that one's Higher Self is adept at using the energy from meltdowns to some purposeful end. Perhaps Soul occasionally induces a meltdown, simply to generate energy for some useful purpose. Perhaps–I hope–the following incident demonstrates an example of this.

Meltdown in Pasadena

IT WAS FOUR o'clock in the morning and to avoid traffic, my wife and I were getting an early start, driving on the Foothill freeway in Pasadena, California, headed upstate to Sonoma. Our exit, which involved the freeway (210) jutting north, was just ahead, an exit I had taken many dozens of times.

As I approached the exit, I could not believe my eyes. There was a curb two meters wide, separating the exit lane from the freeway, which made exiting impossible. I was stupefied, and quickly irritated. "What on Earth was this about? This wasn't fair at all. Com'on!"

I took the next exit, Fair Oaks Avenue, and circled back to give it another try. I couldn't make sense of it and was getting hot. My wife was confused as well. I must have seen it wrong. This was crazy. I got back on the freeway and headed for the exit again as primed-alert as a hawk. The curb was still there! I was stunned, dumbfounded, and my frustration level shot up. This wasn't normal! What was going on? This was personal!

There was no choice but to circle around again as there was no easy alternate route. As I drove back through the streets for a second time, I was fully incensed. The circling around was taking some time, and the early start seemed shot. I screamed out a burst of eyes-shut, clenched-teeth anger for five seconds with all of my available might. After doing so I saw a strange image in my mind's eye for two or three seconds. A man was pointing a gun at a young black couple inside an apartment.

I got on the freeway and headed for the exit for the third time. The curb was still there! I pulled up next to it, drove up and over it on to the exit lane and we were on our way.

Comments: After contemplating this episode, I came to the conclusion that my Higher Self incited my anger, thereby producing enough energy to somehow affect a rescue of that young black couple. I may be wrong and usually am, but that was the best I could come up with. White-hot anger releases tremendous amounts of energy: perhaps the Higher Self is loathe to waste it and may even create it for Its own purposes.

I Can Fly

AFTER TANGLING IN dreams with my shadow manifested as a man, it showed up in this experience as a beautiful young woman. I had the awareness in this dream that I was looking for this witch, who had on several occasions tried to kill me. She was as angry as she was beautiful, with very pale skin and long coal-black hair. While talking with a friend in the room of a large building, I saw her run by the open door, and I took off after her, full speed.

She ran down a stairway that descended in 180 degree turns, and I followed as fast as I could, taking the stairs three and four at a time. Upon turning for the next downward leap, my momentum took me into a large, dark pit. It was a trap! I fell and fell into the pitch-black void, and fear gripped me as the pit seemed bottomless.

Suddenly, a flash hit me like a bolt of electricity: "I can fly!" Immediately I began ascending up and up and out of the pit into brilliant sunshine. I was free!

Comments: While at this time I had gained some experience with the male half of my dark side, I had scant awareness of the female side. Raised in an overwhelmingly male paradigm, my anima was near totally repressed, and while I demonstrated much negative anima behavior, I did not understand what I was doing. Consequently, my only recourse was to transcend this negativity, and that was exactly what the dream was prompting me to do until I could better understand what this component had suffered, and needed.

There was little doubt that this bottled-up part of my shadow was very angry, and its only expression was in negative feminine behavior. It would be years before gaining some light concerning this challenge.

One Cell of the Body

THIS ARCHETYPAL DREAM experience took place in a gigantic male body, which was easily a million kilometers tall. I was a cell in that body, some where near the waist, and I, along with countless other oval-shaped cells in neat rows, comprised the inside surface of a blood vessel which was about ninety cells thick, and deep within the body. I could both see and feel the blood as it coursed over the surface of my body in evenly pulsed waves.

I left my "cell-body" and journeyed outside the gigantic form, buzzing around much like the way a mosquito flies. There were a few others who had left their cells and were drifting about, but surprisingly few.

I gazed upward towards the head of that immense body, which was somehow so far away that one could not just fly up there, and gasped in awe. The sight was so stupendous that any description would fail. The immense head, with tousled golden hair and features like a Greek God, looked slightly upward with thinly parted lips; His beautiful eyes were unfocused, and He had a calm contemplative look on His shining countenance.

Around His head and shoulders was a brilliant radiance of gold-white light, emanating out from His head and forming a massive corona that shone like sunbeams off polished gold; it was simply too large to estimate and glowed in a wondrously beautiful way, with light beams pulsing around within It, and then exploding outward in all directions. An ineffable ecstasy arose within me, and I felt sick with longing to be a part of that immense ocean of light.

With a shock I realized that this incredible vision was comprised of Souls that had left their cells, and gradually made their way up to the top of this enormous Being, becoming part of the wondrous consciousness surrounding this God's head. I realized that joining that colossal Splendor was the goal, not just for me, but for all Creation as well.

Comments: There are many recorded instances of similar visions of this gigantic figure by seekers and teachers of the past, and He is generally ascribed to be the first positive manifestation of God above the lower dual worlds. Sometimes He is known as the Son of the Absolute, or God, in many languages. In Northern India He is often called *Sat Nam* and is a symbolic representative of the Self or Soul at the fifth-plane level, which is generally a neutral transition zone between the lower and higher heavens. This corresponded to my cell's position in the giant form.

This is the level of Self-Realization, generally considered halfway to God-Realization, and Soul at this point receives knowledge of Its missions: the first is to continue on towards God-Realization, the ultimate apotheosis of all eternity, when the Human Soul meets, blends, and becomes one with the Divine Self; the second will involve what Soul, at this level, is presently doing to help God's cause throughout Its vast creation.

When the Human Soul meets Sat Nam, It has already met and become one with the inner consciousness (Soul) of Its Astral, Causal, and Higher Mental bodies, and is ready to meet Its own Higher Self, the Child of Its own Divine Self. This is Self-Realization. In Hindu terms, the Jiva meets Its own *Atman* (Higher Self), child of Its own Paramatman, the Supreme Self or Christ Self; in Christian parlance, this is Salvation, being born of the Spirit.

The vision also works when interpreting the gigantic figure (which a woman may see as female) as at the very top of Creation, instead of mid-way. When Soul is trapped in the lower worlds, to merge with Sat Nam, or attain Self-Realization, is the goal. Once that has happened, the goal becomes to meet and merge with the Supreme Self, or God-Realization. Technically, the term God-Realization is a misnomer, since no Soul ever realizes God. This step should be called Divine-Self Realization, Paramatman-Realization, or Christ-Self Realization.

That one is a cell of God's body is a universal concept present in all paths, and Saint Paul's quote in Acts of the *Christian Bible* frames it beautifully: "For in Him we live, and move, and have our being...." And while Soul may be one tiny little cell in a body beyond all reckoning, It may interface with the consciousness of whatever level It reaches, eventually becoming one with all Creation, and finally, becoming Creation Itself.

When Soul realizes Its core identity as the Holy Spirit, Soul is everywhere, as the Holy Spirit is everywhere, and Soul or Atman is everything, as the Holy Spirit is everything. This does not include the Ultimate Absolute, as IT is completely separate from Creation.

The Court of Sat Nam

THIS INNER EXPERIENCE happened at roughly the same time. I became aware while dreaming that I was visiting the Court of Sat Nam, Lord of the fifth plane. The palace was circular, and inside the main hall were tiers rising in concentric circles from a center stage. The stage held a circular, red, cushioned dais that rose two meters from the floor.

The tiers were totally filled with Souls standing reverently in total silence. I stood several rows up from the bottom, and I giggled to myself because it seemed like I was awfully young to be there. The individuals, wearing vaporous forms, stood silently and were of every description; it was apparent that they were from planets and planes all over the lower creations. One in front and to the side of me had a large translucent, trunk-like appendage coming out of the back of his head that reached down close to the floor.

Others had long robes with cowls and as those in front of me faced the stage, I could not see their faces. There was no way to tell the sex of those who were in attendance, and I assumed that there were all manner of differing classifications present. The dais was empty.

Comments: The central point of this experience is that the dais was empty. Self-Realization requires the human Soul, which has met, merged, and identified Itself as Its own Higher Self, the Atman, taking center stage, metaphorically, and seating Itself upon the dais. At this point, Soul has already assumed the dais, or throne, of the lower four heavens. It is time to merge and identify as the Atman, the Higher Self. One does not have to Become It; one must realize that one is It.

Mind Versus Soul

PERHAPS ONE OF the greatest difficulties that seekers face in understanding esoteric Spirituality, is in discerning the differences between truth in the lower dual heavens, and truth in the higher heavens; it is also the same difference between mind and Soul. The differences are so extreme as to be opposite, as though the lower heaven's truth is a mirror image of the higher heaven's truth: accurate in detail, but totally reversed. Most of the Spiritual teaching today, and all of the religions and philosophies, are propagating truths from the lower heavens. This is not necessarily wrong as this is their state of consciousness.

Perhaps, in the West, the term used to describe the wondrous consciousness attainable on the third and fourth levels of heaven, which are still dual and negative, is Cosmic Consciousness; in the East it is *Samadhi*. Earth's greatest writers, poets, and religious teachers have celebrated this high state of consciousness, which teaches the sisterhood and brotherhood of all humankind, and the unadulterated unity of all things. Saints and mystics experiencing the visions and revelations that attend this state report encounters with blazing lights, and melting into oneness with all life. They often feel they are one with God and teach so.

Poets, like Yeats, Whitman, Wordsworth, Keats, Shelly, Byron, Shakespeare, Emerson, Thoreau, and so many others, perceive the one God in everything, and that everything is God.

Many call this state enlightenment and claim it is union with God. Others teach that this collective union is the end of individuality, and that one joins the "All" in such a way as to never have existed as a separate entity.

Those who have attained this state of consciousness feel that they are at the very top of Creation and are immortal; they would never believe that they are one with the lower dual powers. Many religions have established paradises for their followers in the second, third, and fourth levels of heaven, which are beautiful and happy places.

Many goodly Souls from these regions incarnate on Physical Plane planets like Earth to help and teach humanity. However, the beliefs these Souls are living by and elucidating are far from God's truth in the higher heavens. It is not that they are totally wrong; it is just that they are stepping-stones to the deeper reality, much like addition and subtraction are steps to learning higher math.

The higher heavens are concerned with becoming an individual, not in joining some undifferentiated union with God. Of course all of God's Body is unified, but God needs realized Souls as channels to run His vast universes and that is what the higher heavens prepare Soul to do: become a co-worker with the Divine.

While it is true that God is in all, as the poets have testified to, notice that they are always seeing God in the outside world; to attain the higher heavens, one looks for God's Spirit inside, and then realizes one's identity as It.

Of course the "Light" is still present, but a relationship with the "Sound," the audible Power of God, becomes one's very Savior and Self. Without a relationship with this aspect of the Holy Spirit it is impossible to go further.

Instead of melting away into infinity, one congeals as Soul, Spirit, and the Divine Self, which is the pinnacle, the very apotheosis of individuality; and, rather than Soul fantasizing Itself as at the top of Creation, it learns that Self-Realization is the virtual beginning of Its sojourn into the purely positive God-Planes.

In addition, those from the Soul plane no longer need methods, teachers or symbols. Who needs a method to become what you already are? Who needs a teacher when you have become one? And who needs symbols when one has become what the symbols symbolize?

The state of awareness that attends Self-Realization on the fifth plane of heaven and above is termed the *Nirvikalpa* in the Hindu lexicon, and is as far above enlightenment, or Samadhi, as the Sun's light is above the Moon's. The Nirvikalpa is the Atman's or Higher Self's consciousness, so to speak, instead of the Soul/mind's, and represents a level of deep inner perception and knowingness that the Soul through mind could never fathom. It is a deep knowingness that dispels all doubt and negativity. One is a realized Soul and above the dual worlds, and one knows it.

That there is tremendous confusion about these differences between Cosmic Conscious and Self-Realization is understandable, in light of the fact that one out of ninety-nine teachers have experienced complete Self-Realization, although those from the fourth level of heaven have begun the process.

There are many stages and steps in the process of realizing one's Self at the fifth plane of heaven, or Atman level, and if an evolved Soul has been through this realization before in previous lives, it may go relatively quickly over a span of years; however, if it is the first time that Soul is working on Self-Realization, there is much time involved.

Earth is God's first grade, and it is easy for students to be confused about the higher grades, especially when pupils from the varying grades above are disseminating so much contradictory information about what they are learning. By graduation time, it is all straightened out.

The Narrow Gate

THERE ARE MANY ways to travel outside of the body; some of them simply involve leaving the body consciousness, others involve leaving the physical body entirely. As Soul learns to travel apart from Its body consciousness, It is doing so "inside Itself," exploring Its own universes and planes; at the same time, teachers and helpers are aiding It in learning how to travel "outside" in the macrocosm.

By the time Self-Realization occurs, Soul is adept at leaving the body without help, going inside to go outside into the larger universes of God, the same universes that it has a perfect replica of inside Its own Self that It has explored. During the process of completing the realization that It is the Atman or Higher Self, it will learn to stay and operate out of the body permanently, and run it from a distance, or from a different dimension. Soul is anxious to do this as it prevents becoming trapped in the body, something that can occur when the body is undergoing emotional disturbances.

Not only are there many ways for Soul to leave the body, there are many ways to look at each way of leaving. This vision demonstrated one such point of view of one such way of leaving the body.

I was sleeping soundly when I suddenly became aware that I was positioned near the solar plexus, and that I was gathering all of my energy, not only from all over my body, but from everything that I owned as well: clothes in the dresser, pictures on the walls, small appliances, the television, and personal items.

The energy flows were represented by red lines moving from my personal belongings to a spot just below my rib cage. The biggest band, about the diameter of my wrist, came from my car in the back yard. When the energy transfer was complete, the lines disappeared, and the entire episode had lasted no more than a half-minute.

Somehow, all of this energy, most of it from my body, was condensed to pinprick size, and I shot up through the *chakras* and out through the *Crown Chakra* at the top of the head. I was conscious of the fact that this shrinkage of size was necessary to get through the chakras, especially the last one.

As soon as I was out of the body I began expanding my Spirit, and as I was living in Los Angeles at the time, I rapidly enveloped the entire city and its one hundred-plus suburbs. Below me, in the dark of night, the Astral light currents were rushing to and fro at right angles to each other. All was silent and peaceful. Suddenly, a thought occurred to me.

Recently, in my waking life, I had applied for a job with a large company. It was a real long shot with little hope of success, and I thought of this as my Spirit drifted over the city. I knew that all I had to do was reach a finger down with the quickest little touch, and everything would immediately be arranged, making the job mine for the asking. However, a strong feeling arose within me cautioning against such a move, and I refrained from acting.

The next thing that I was aware of was that I had reentered the body, and all of the energy I had amassed began streaming out from my center to its former place or function. As the light energy flowed out from me to various centers, my consciousness was progressively jolted down in stages: some were small downgrades, others really large, and it was a terrible feeling as though one were losing their mind.

This dispersion seemed to go on inordinately long: down, down, and down again, and just when I thought it had to be over, down again, perhaps a total of fifteen times, until it was all the way down to what I experience as the human consciousness; it felt like total ignorance and darkness and seemed as though I had lost 99 percent of my awareness.

Comments: One of the immediate effects of this vision was to nudge me towards caring less about my possessions: I saw with my own eyes how much energy I had in them. These bands of energy, connecting Soul to various people and objects, hold Soul imprisoned like a fly in a spider web, which makes it impossible to fly.

As to shrinking the consciousness to pinprick size in order to get through the Crown Chakra, I am reminded of the quote by the Christ in Jesus: "Because strait is the gate, and narrow is the way, which leadeth unto life, and few there be who find it." There are those that interpret this verse as referring to this requirement for leaving through the Crown Chakra.

Theodore Roethke has a profound poem titled, "The Waking," in which he pens: "I wake to sleep, and take my waking slow…I learn by going where I have to go." This is true regarding out-of-body travel. One's waking state becomes like sleep compared to the luminous consciousness experienced when out-of-body, and the going, when awake here on Earth, seems agonizingly slow; what may be created instantly in the higher dimensions may take lifetimes here on Earth.

When I returned to the body and began redistributing my consciousness, it was very much like the scene in the movie, *2001*, when Hal the computer is systematically unplugged and experiences the gradual loss of consciousness. Before my consciousness had been "unplugged," not only could I spread my Spirit to any size desired, I had power over all below me and could control it if desired.

Demon

THIS DISCONCERTING DREAM happened one night when I became conscious of being in a pitch-dark room. Suddenly, a force began tossing me around the room, bouncing me of the walls, ceiling, and floor. It was absolutely terrifying! A voice began speaking: "Mark, you have a demon. Many Spiritual seekers have demons. The greater the seeker, the greater the demon."

The scene shifted and I found myself riding a bicycle, being chased by a young girl, perhaps seven or eight years old, also on a bicycle. She was angry and ugly, green in color, and as I glanced back, she vomited a vile stream of army-green puke. She was gaining on me, and as she came up behind my bicycle, I reached back to grab her hand, planning to throw her violently against an approaching wall. Just as I was about to grab her, she stabbed me in the hand with a little cuticle scissors.

Comments: My father believed in harsh physical discipline, often applied, and consequently, I hated him with a passion for many years. This created an artificial elemental, fed by intense anger that grew increasingly powerful over the years; its very Soul was the hate I had for my father. This is how demons are created, and the accumulated energy can be so powerful that it takes years to release, if ever. It does not diminish of itself, and one needs tremendous understanding to heal whatever created the problem. Until that time, the demon will wreck havoc any way it can, looking for opportunities to discharge its venom.

In this instance, the little green girl with the scissors was demonstrating one avenue the demon was using to spew out its animosity: it was in little derogatory remarks or cuts, and in a waspish, negative feminine way that was intended to make my victims feel the pain that I, and by extension the demon, felt. And this was by no means the demon's only avenue of release; unfortunately, it was just one of many.

I had several experiences over years in attempting to disarm and release this demon's energies. It is something that must be done gradually as the energies involved are huge; there is a danger in releasing these forces too quickly lest the individual snap or break down.

Sometimes these accumulated energies are called engrams, which are like miniature demons, created by painful and humiliating incidents. They can fester in one's aura for years, blocking healthy expression in the area affected.

Ironically, if one works on healing the problem, these energies are released and come out through the individual, prompting the very behavior they are attempting to resolve. Understanding and forgiveness are the principle means of healing these problems.

Dreams will help in understanding what one was feeling when these problems were created. Often times, the person remembers the painful incident, but has repressed or suppressed the intensity of their feelings created by the experience; dreams will bring it back exactly, which is especially helpful for situations created in early childhood that are out of conscious memory's reach.

Dreams will also provide the solution, if the person is not grasping it consciously. This often involves accepting responsibility for one's own part in creating the situation. Usually one is experiencing the return of their own karma, something they created in this or previous lifetimes. One has to fess up.

In addition, one will have to forgive all concerned, including themselves. There is nothing that cannot be understood, and there is nothing that cannot be forgiven.

The Law

ONE SUNNY AFTERNOON I accompanied a friend on a short visit to a lakeside cabin. He had a small business matter to attend to with the owner, and while waiting for him I roamed the shoreline of the property. There on a nearby dock I noticed a fishing rod.

I had grown up in a fishing family, but I had given up fishing years before out of principle, deciding I did not want to end their physical incarnation unless necessary for food. Fish are more evolved than most people would ever suspect; those who keep aquariums know what I mean.

The wait got a little longer than expected, and I decided to take a few casts with the rod and reel, which had a big artificial lure attached to the end of the line. After a couple of casts, I got a hard strike, and I could tell by the pull that it was probably a northern pike. After a half-minute fight the fish got off the hook and escaped, and as my friend had finished his business and was approaching, I put the rod and reel back on the dock and we left.

The very next day I went to a public beach on the very same lake for a refreshing swim. I dove in the cold water and swam out near the buoys separating the boat traffic from the swimmers and began treading water.

Suddenly, a large fish hit against my chest with incredible force and bit my right nipple with a vengeance, drawing blood and turning the water red near my chest. The pain was intense and I swam for shore.

It's probable that the fish thought it the end of a worm, and from his point of view, I was probably too big to see. I drove home, dressed the wound, and sat down for a "session" to contemplate what had happened. How fun!

Comments: It was not hard to figure out what had happened: I didn't have to; the Holy Force placed it into my human consciousness. By casting for a fish with the rod and reel I had violated my own law, and retribution was swift. It is probable, if I intuited this correctly, that I experienced the exact same amount of pain as I inflicted on the fish. And if some authority told me that it was the very same fish–although it doesn't matter–I would not even bat an eye.

This incident was a great lesson on the concept of making one's own laws and living by them. If I had not decided on principle to avoid fishing, that miniature "jaws" would have never attacked me, or so I believe.

Carl Jung boiled all mental disease down to one original cause: not doing what one thinks is right. By doing wrong in one's own eyes, a disassociation is formed, one side of the mind arguing with the other side. As James, in the *Christian Bible* states: "A double-minded man is unstable in all his ways."

This principle is law in the higher worlds, and is the basis for weighing Soul and Its actions. This principle also modifies karma in the lower heavens, as there are times one does wrong but for good reasons, or does not know a certain action is wrong.

If one attempts with sincerity to do what is right in their eyes, they may or may not have their deepest truth, but they either have it or are on the right road to discover it. They will avoid the unwanted consequences of not following one's Inner Guide, and will reap the desired rewards for aligning themselves with It.

Digging for Truth

ONE AFTERNOON I brought the Bhagavad-Gita, a Hindu religious work, along with a shovel, up to a contemplation spot I was preparing in the foothills of the San Gabriel Mountains. I had leveled a small space a third of the way up a steep foothill that was hidden and remote, and with a little more landscaping it would be a miniature paradise.

I had also begun reading the Bhagavad-Gita and was very impressed with it; it seemed to me that they were rather accurately describing the realized states, and I eagerly looked forward to finishing the book, written by the legendary Vyasa.

I laid the book on a bench-like boulder and began to move some soil around with the shovel, landscaping an area the size of a small room. I was debating whether I should plant a little grass when a loud crashing noise high above me caught my attention. It sounded like a small avalanche and it was headed my way. Due to the steep cliff-side I could not see what was coming a couple of hundred meters above me, and it continued smashing and crashing for several seconds while I waited to see what would happen. I dropped the shovel, stood back several meters, and looked up, waiting.

Suddenly, a large rock the size and shape of a watermelon, bounced into view high above me, somersaulting through the air straight for me. I stepped to the side and tensely waited to make a dive, if needed, out of the boulder's way. Bam! The rock landed squarely on the Bhagavad-Gita and bounced directly into the metal blade of the shovel with a clang so loud it sounded as though someone had struck a large gong with a maul.

Somewhat shaken, I picked up the book. Two perfect circles were deeply imprinted and symmetrically placed under the title on the cover. I examined the rock that had landed on it and discovered on one end the two protrusions that matched the indentations on the book.

Comments: When initially contemplating this experience, I felt that the large ringing collision of the shovel and rock was the Holy Spirit telling me to keep digging in the Bhagavad-Gita. As to the two perfectly placed circles on the cover, I was not so sure what to make of it, but I knew it was significant. After finishing the book I believe that I was shown the answer: the Bhagavad- Gita is dual, and of the lower heavens.

It is true that this scripture contains many high states of consciousness, especially in describing a realized person. By realized it is meant that the individual has attained Self- Realization and established themselves on at least the fifth level of heaven above the lower dual worlds. But while describing this state with some insight, the book has little understanding about how to attain it. They offer a host of rules, methods, and practices that an aspirant is supposed to perform, but none of them would get one further than the mental plane.

One cannot "get" Self-Realization, nor is a master or guru able to give this experience: it is given to one by the Holy Spirit when one is ready, and all the purifying in the world, combined with every good method known, will not produce this high state. What will? Give up being the potter, and become the clay. Surrender everything to the Higher Self, and let It guide one in all. One does not try to attain It; one realizes they are It as the term denotes. Seeking it chases it away; declaring it affirms it.

The Bhagavad-Gita does not realize this: it would have one try to become what they already are, further distancing them from the realization that they are Atman now. A seeker's basic hypothesis is that they do not have it, and that is exactly what they are creating. Eventually, Soul Itself will have to accept and declare this state to create it.

The amazing precision with which the Higher Self created this experience is another testament to Its total control over every aspect of life. There is never an end to it. I brought home the rock; it weighed twenty-two kilos.

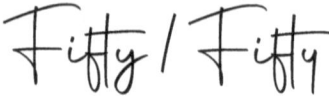

Fifty / Fifty

I HAD JUST FINISHED up a delicious Chinese dinner and I opened the accompanying fortune cookie. It read: "Your good traits outweigh your bad."

I laughed and crumpled the fortune while I thought to myself, I'm a lot further along than that, maybe 90 per cent good and 10 percent bad. Man alive, I've been on the path for twenty years.

The following morning, jutst before waking up, I was on the receiving end of an explanation from some authority, presumably my Higher Self. The voice said, "Mark, you really did just make the half-way point to where your good and bad traits are evenly balanced. And by the way, Mark, your bad traits are much worse than other people's bad traits."

Comments: This was a sobering reality check that I obviously needed. Apart from my own personal failures, it brings to mind the concept of balance, and of course this applies to one's Spiritual pursuits as well: one's Spiritual successes and failures must balance. Jesus refused to be called a good man, declaring that "…only the Father is good." Where does that leave the rest of us?

Transcendence

IT HAD BEEN a rough three years, and I was doing a poor job of maintaining my attitude. It seemed as though nearly everything was "going south," and I was starting to feel down and depressed. As I was in the bathroom getting ready for work, I accidentally dropped a hand mirror on the floor, cracking it within the frame and creating a loud noise. Upon picking the mirror up, I noticed that the breakage had created a perfect line-drawing of a duck ascending in flight. The message seemed apparent: transcend, fly above it. I mustered all of my energy and did what I could to create a Spiritual thrill; it was weak. However, a very feminine voice inside my head said, "Good, Mark, that's the idea."

I did my best to go on from there and did not look back.

Comments: There is very little one can do to change or avoid their basic karmic lot, but one has tremendous latitude in how they respond to said events. Ideally, one wants to regard anything and everything from the highest state of consciousness possible as one's attitude determines much of what happens. Those that play the victim card and blame society and others for their predicament are simply not evolved enough to take responsibility for their own actions. "You reap what you sow" is not just a fancy metaphor.

There is a comforting thought that can be relied on by a Spiritual seeker: everything that happens will be necessary and for the seeker's good. There will be no unnecessary accidents or tragedies, although the student may at times feel like questioning that. Clearing karmic debts is difficult, but they are debts and it is wonderful to have them paid.

An additional benefit of consciously cooperating with the "Force" is that one's Higher Self may modify hard karma by spreading it out into several smaller payments, rather than one big tragedy; non-seekers do not enjoy such a privilege and fall under the law of accidents. If one does not think that the Spiritual Forces are capable of "hardball," check out the news or stop by the local morgue.

The feminine voice in my head was my anima acting as though "she" was my mother, and although her rare intrusions could be annoying, she was invested in my success. She was just the type to remind one of the oft-repeated aphorism: "When you have lemons, make lemonade."

As simple as this sounds, it is one of the keys to Spiritual success. A winning attitude incorporates optimism, detachment, strength of will, and understanding. It is an accurate barometer of an individual's Spiritual health and their ability to transcend. If it is true that one literally creates one's own life through thought, feeling, and imagination, why would one want a bad temperament?

What Matters?

IN THIS DREAM experience, I was a member of a small discussion group, and although I did not see anyone, it seemed as though several of us were positioned in a circle listening to an Instructor, who was probably my Higher Self. It seemed as though I had become aware mid-lesson, with the Teacher in the middle of making a point. I focused intently.

The telepathic-like communication continued, "It doesn't matter if you're a man or a woman. It doesn't matter what religion you are or if you are not religious. It is no matter what race or ethnicity you are, or if you are young, middle-aged, or old, and it certainly is not germane how intelligent you are, or whether or not you are educated; if you cannot read or write, so what."

At this last statement I felt a twinge, as I had always counted a decent education as an advantage, and here the Teacher had just panned it as of no consequence.

The Instructor continued: "It is of no concern if you are married or not, and your sexual orientation couldn't matter less. Sickness, disease, drugs and drink are beside the point, and whether you are sexually active or not, who cares? If you believe in a Creator, and profess your faith, good for you, but it matters not. Purity matters even less. Purity comes *after* you realize God."

It was about this time that I started to really wonder, what did matter? It seemed like the Teacher had named about everything I could think of, and I had joined the group in mid-discussion. Maybe a bunch of other things had already been eliminated before I had arrived.

Then the Teacher dropped a bombshell that really floored me: "I don't care what plane of heaven you're from, and it doesn't matter a whit whether you're evolved or not."

"Holy Moly!" I exclaimed to myself, I'd always prided myself on thinking I was somewhat evolved, and the Teacher had just totally discounted it, saying it was a non-issue.

I could tell that the entire group listening to this were perplexed and was aching to know what the Teacher was going to say mattered or, did nothing matter?

"What matters?" the Instructor said, pausing for a moment, "The only thing that matters is what is going through your head right now."

Comments: The principles that govern attention are mathematical and precise and well-known to science: attention put on some "object" is forceful in proportion to the narrowness of its focus; the amount of attention fixed on a thought is proportional to its power; one's inner force can be measured by one's power of attention; the attention focused on one thing shuts out other things; the thoughts and ideas that move one to action are the thoughts and ideas that possess one's attention. One may comprehend in a second why love is so important; it is the most powerful attention there is.

One beautiful result of putting the attention on Spiritual things is that it diminishes that power given the "world": bad habits, bad thoughts and bad feelings gradually become starved for energy, as one's Spiritual life becomes "fat." Energy given to one's Spiritual life is cumulative and when amassed to a required amount, manifests the desired result; it could be likened to a chemical reaction. No amount of attention given to one's Spiritual pursuit is ever wasted, even if it is only forty-five seconds at a red light. "Thou wilt keep him in perfect peace whose mind is stayed on thee...."

A second consideration contained in the experience is that nothing may be going through one's head at all. This may arguably be better than placing the attention on some worthy thing and is the goal of countless aspirants all over the globe. If one can stop thought, contact with one's Higher Self is imminent, and one can "know" things unavailable to common thinking. Of course, both the placing and withdrawal of attention are necessary for the Spiritual life.

A third consideration, and no doubt the most important, is that life is always lived in the here and now. True Salvation or realization is not something that occurs after death in some paradise. True Salvation is the ability to live in the Spiritual consciousness right now, and in any future now, the same thing will have to be done, no matter the place. What is in one's head right now determines everything, and it is always right now. Of course eternity is now, and it has been forever. "Now" is the correct definition of eternity.

A correct placing of attention will correct any needed changes in the things that people believe matter.

To place attention on Spiritual things, or to stop attention altogether, is difficult in the beginning. The mind wants no part of either. It is easy to determine if one is a God-lover: simply add up the time and attention one spends with God during an average day, versus the time and attention spent on family, job, entertainment, mate, and life's details.

Of course, the time spent on Spirituality should far outweigh all of the other things put together. One does not have to have the attention on trivial worldly responsibilities, even while one is doing them. "For where your treasure is, there will your heart be also."

Death Ward

I HAD BEEN INJURED and I knew that a recovery was going to take a long time, if ever. I was down. That night in a dream, I found myself on a gurney being wheeled into a hospital ward that contained dozens of dying and diseased patients. They were all on gurneys, in tiered rows, rising up out of sight towards some invisible ceiling.

The consciousness in that room was the lowest, sickest, filthiest, pity-filled display of negativity that I have ever witnessed. It made depression seem like ecstasy in comparison. The patients were moaning and groaning; sobbing and weeping; screaming and ranting; cursing and swearing; pleading and begging. It was a nightmarish feeling beyond words, and I woke up in a drenching sweat, spitting continuously as though I were trying to expel some evil thing.

Comments: After having this dream I vowed to take the high road. It was as if the "Force" said to me–referring to the death ward–"Mark, do you really want to go there?" No sane person would, although many millions are living in there every day, and their negative consciousness recreates their horror continuously. No doubt tragic occurrences test the ability to transcend and maintain a healthy attitude, but what is the option? Usually, there is little one can do to change tragic events, but one has immense latitude as to their response, and Spiritual help is always available.

All Creation goes to God for refuge; there is none other.

As One

ONE NIGHT AS I lay sleeping, I found myself walking in a beautiful surreal landscape with lovely canals interspersed among flowered greenswards. Suddenly the vision of a face appeared high above covering a large portion of the sky; it was my own visage and looked like John's vision in *Revelations* of "...one like unto the Son of Man."

Out of "my" mouth came a sword, followed by various-sized packages. They were wrapped in paper and string, flowing in a column out into the surrounding ethers.

All at once, I was the giant figure in the sky, and I looked down on my other Self walking along the canals far below; there was not a smidgen of interior dialogue; I was simply watching.

Abruptly, I was the figure on the ground again gazing up at the immense countenance above. There was not any thought at this end as well, and I simply stared above in awe.

Again I switched places and became the colossal vision in the heavens, surveying the scene below. I watched the Self on the ground impassively.

Comments: This vision occurred some little time after visiting the Court of Sat Nam and represented the process of becoming one with the Atman or Higher Self: Self-Realization. The Sikhs refer to this plane as *Satya Loka,* and while the Lord of this world has many names, there is usually a sharp distinction made between this world and the next. While this region is often called the first plane of heaven, it being above the dual worlds, technically the next plane, *Alakh Loka,* is the first level that is positive, unlike the neutral transition zone Satya Loka, which is positioned between the lower dual worlds and higher positive planes of heaven.

The packages flowing from the mouth symbolized the various states of consciousness accompanying and comprising this field of consciousness; the unwrapping of them, and what they represented, lay just ahead. The oneness of the Human Soul and the Higher Self at this level, the fifth plane of heaven, was stressed; this step is usually called Jivan Mukti in Hinduism, Nirvana in Buddhism, Salvation in Christianity, and experiencing it called into question the various schools of thought (e.g. *Visistadvaita*) that consider this event impossible while still in a human body.

Perhaps, as many saints have reported, it must be accomplished while in a human body, as it is the Human Soul, along with Soul in the Astral, Lower Mental, Causal, Higher Mental Body, and as Atman that is liberated. This process continues inward, with the realization of Soul as Spirit, Light and Sound, and eventually, the Divine Self. This is the infinite dream and destination of every Soul created.

These events in Soul's journey are accompanied by signature experiences: one sees them with their own physical consciousness' eyes, and the reality, the "realness" of them carries such an enormous impact that much work is needed to prepare for these experiences lest Soul become unhinged, let alone the physical consciousness.

The human consciousness has little to do with engineering Spiritual realizations and besides an embarrassing incompetence, is unworthy to the nth degree. Its job is to maintain contact with the Higher Selves through devotions and attempt to follow Its direction. This done, one is along for a glorious ride: the ride of rides!

There are schools of thought that consider Self-Realization the first initiation, as it is a convenient starting point. Other paths place it much higher, but whatever the number, Soul has realized Itself and is liberated from the lower heavens. In Christian parlance, Soul has been born of the Spirit, reentered the Garden of Eden (heaven) and eaten from the tree of life (immortality). Soul at this point is the prodigal Son/Daughter who has returned home to a glorious welcome from the Mother/Father.

In Hindu thought, although many competing schools differ on particulars, the Human Soul (*Surat*) has realized It is Jivatman, which in turn has realized It is Atman; the Human Soul is halfway to realizing Itself as Paramatman, and by extension, *Brahman*, which is a refinement and expansion of the parallel realization already experienced.

Soul's realization is accompanied by an enormous expansion of consciousness and awareness that is available all the way down to the human consciousness. Not only does one increasingly comprehend the utter magnificence of one's own Higher Selves, in addition, one also begins to perceive the horrifying depths of their own darkness. It may seem indeed that the real work to clean house has just begun. Hercules' fifth labor was to clean the Augean Stables (purification) in only one day (lifetime).

The vision of one's Higher Self in the sky is archetypal; every Soul who experiences Self-Realization at this level appears the same way, albeit graced with a different visage. Out of respect, I will not describe it further.

Multi-Pointed Consciousness

EARLY ONE MORNING, just before awakening, I had the awareness of being about to enter the body consciousness. I entered the body and awakened it.

From the mind and Human Soul's point of view, I awakened remembering my awareness of just being outside the body. However, I had barely cleared my mind when abruptly I again left the body consciousness. Then, after only five seconds, I came back into waking consciousness.

From a human consciousness point of view none of this was under my control, but since I had been awakened before the quick transition back and forth, it offered the perfect opportunity to grab something of what my consciousness was like on the other side. I strained with all my might to remember anything of what I had just experienced in my other consciousness, much like anyone trying to remember a just-finished dream.

For the most part, I could grab nothing; I was like an ant trying to remember what it was like to be human. However, I did have an image of watching fifty television sets at once and interacting simultaneously with the programs on each one of them.

Comments: This "happening" offered much clarity on out-of-body consciousness experiences, and it disproved many of the claims made by those peddling conscious travel out-of-body.

I had never really considered the term "multi-pointed consciousness" until this event, but it is an accurate definition of doing several things at once. Of course, on Earth one is fortunate to be able to handle one thing at a time; on the other side, the sky is the limit. The capacity to handle multiple things at once increases commensurate to the consciousness one is in: Human Soul, Soul in The Astral, Lower Mental, Causal, Higher Mental, Soul, Spirit and on up to the Divine Self. Not only can these higher centers of one's Self handle incredible amounts of interfacing simultaneously, an evolved Soul may be running multiple bodies spread out over the time track and universes like a net, trolling for experience and Souls that need help.

This gets into numbers too incredible to believe. It is common knowledge in some circles that when a high emissary of the Almighty incarnates, that Soul is virtually everywhere at once, and of course, every atom, body, Soul, and Spirit in existence is being "run" by one Being.

It becomes obvious why the human mind cannot be conscious of Soul's adventures in other dimensions: its capacity is so very low that Soul must communicate Its lessons and messages in easy to interpret symbols and metaphors that the human consciousness can decipher. A poor human being would be fused immediately if actually experiencing Soul's consciousness. However, there is a bit of an exception: mystical experiences.

Somehow, Soul does impart incredibly advanced perceptions, when desired, all the way down to the human mind, in visions that are not a dream. If Soul so chooses to impart an experience to the human consciousness, the depth of perception it is possible for one to receive is staggering. It is still miniscule compared with what the Higher Self is experiencing; nonetheless, it is beyond all normal waking experience, and may take years to properly assimilate.

Death Clinic

I WAS IN A clinic-like building in this dream, and I was preparing to die. I was a young man in good health, but the time had come to leave. The place was nearly deserted; I had seen a nurse walk across a distant hallway but all was silent.

No one was there to see me off, and the "feel" of things was impersonal and rather cold, like this was simply business as usual. As soon as I was finished showering I was going to lie on the table and leave.

While standing under the shower, I had a brief attack of a disquieting thought. I was going to die, and nobody cared in the least. But I brushed it aside as sentimental gibberish and finished up the shower.

Comments: Whether this was technically a dream or not, I do not know, but it seemed, as most dreams do, more real than when awake. I believe my Higher Self was sharing Its view of the process, reconfirming the simplicity and naturalness of "death" or "translation."

How Soul goes through this process depends on the Soul's evolvement, as there are huge differences in what Souls at various levels and grades experience. The higher the Soul, the more control of death is possible, and highly evolved Human Souls simply merge with their Higher Self at death of the body without loss of consciousness.

Less evolved Souls have no control of the process and are often unconscious for a time before entering a dream life that, in effect, works off the energies and effects of their preceding life. Some call this journey purgatory, and it is richly detailed in the *Tibetian Book of the Dead*.

After this process is complete, which is very detailed and progressive, and is totally determined by Soul's individual karma, Soul is ready for reincarnation. Some Souls enjoy accumulated good karma and may spend time on the second, third, or fourth level of heaven for incredibly long times before incarnating; others, more anxious to proceed, bank good karma for Spiritual opportunities and incarnate as soon as possible.

Of course, there are many Souls between the high and the low that experience multiple variations of the process between incarnations. Those who are midway through the third level of heaven are beginning to wake up, to see the big picture and where they fit in. They learn how to access past lives, what their karmas are, and begin to consciously participate in their own Spiritual evolution.

The lower dual worlds are a nursery for Souls young in experience. There are uncountable quadrillions of angels, masters, teachers, helpers and elementals tending this nursery, and as channels for the Highest, they shower love and understanding in prodigious amounts on these inexperienced Nomads, preparing them to some day become responsible citizens of God's Kingdom. Death is a wonderful illusion that the Holy Power uses to Its advantage; it incentivizes Souls in myriad ways to learn, to improve, and to make the most of the "now."

> *So teach us to number your days, that we may apply our hearts to wisdom.*
>
> (Psalms 90:12)

Chacmool

ONE AFTERNOON I joined a tour at the Los Angeles County Museum of Art featuring Mesoamerican artifacts. There were beautiful examples of *Mayan, Toltec* and *Aztec* craftsmanship: pottery, masks, obsidian knives, jade carvings, weapons, and the like.

The tour participants slowly walked single file down a rope-lined aisle fronting the exhibits, and gasps of appreciation were common. While waiting for the line to move, I glanced ahead, and what I saw froze me in my tracks: five meters ahead was a large stone statue on the floor of a male warrior lying on his back. It was a *chacmool*, and while I did not know at that time what it was called, I knew exactly what it was and what it was used for: human sacrifice.

Chacmools are sculptures of a reclining figure, usually but not always on its back, and either containing a bowl on its belly for human hearts or other sculpted chambers for body parts. The head is usually turned ninety degrees to the side.

This one had a large chamber like a bathtub where the stomach and chest of the sculpture should be, and was used to hold the sacrificial victim: it had the sickest, most foul vibrations I have ever experienced; one could still hear, very clearly, the victims screaming. The hollowed out chamber was horribly stained!

When I saw the chacmool up ahead of my place in line, I was totally thunderstruck, and I experienced a multi-faceted déjà vu of a past lifetime. Judging by the style of the chacmool, it may have been near Chichen Itza, Mexico, a thousand years ago, when human sacrifice was an everyday occurrence. As I stood staring at the chacmool, I experienced the exact same awareness and feelings as when I had seen it long ago for the first time in Central America.

"A group of about thirty of us were on the run from government soldiers, and the soldiers had just exited the small temple complex we were arriving at, leaving behind a dozen corpses that had been sacrificed to *Acolnahuacutl;* their chests bore gaping wounds where their hearts had been cut out. We did not believe in the government or the official religion, and if caught, we would be sacrificed. The mood was grim, and the barbarity of the priests and soldiers seemed surreal. We had been on the run for a long time."

The line began moving again, awaking me from a deep reflection, and after a few minutes I arrived at the chacmool. On it was a card explaining what it was. It read: "This Chacmool, discovered in Mexico, was used in religious ceremonies. Archeologists are divided on whether it was used for human sacrifice."

Comments: Here is a short passage from Wordsworth's much longer poem, *Ode: Intimations of Immortality From Recollections of Early Childhood:*

> "Our birth is but a sleep and a forgetting:
> The Soul that rises with us, our life's Star,
> Hath had elsewhere its setting,
> And cometh from afar:
> Not in entire forgetfulness,
> And not in utter nakedness,
> But trailing clouds of glory do we come
> From God who is our home:"

There has been much written concerning reincarnation, and other than a handful of general observations, I will let other writers dwell on it more extensively. The first is a suggestion for those who are unsure of its authenticity.

If one is curious as to whether they have lived before, one might ask their Higher Self for experiences that corroborate it. If one is generally sincere, and is neutral enough to accept reincarnation, one's Higher Self will oblige one at the proper time.

Part of the difficulty in recalling the past, or "reremembering," as Plato likes to term it, is that each new lifetime brings with it a new physical body, a new Astral Body, and a new *Manas* or lower Mind Body. In addition, the Human Soul has Its memory wiped; this provides an entirely fresh start but makes recall of the past more difficult. Add to this a culture that conditions its members to disbelieve reincarnation and it is small wonder people cannot remember anything. In large parts of the East, recall of past lives is very common.

This particular déjà vu seemed to be triggered by observing the exact same memorable thing as in a past life. As chacmools vary widely in appearance, I have no doubt that the one in the exhibit was exactly the same one I saw in an earlier incarnation, and my reaction, I believe, also matched my earlier response. The exact repetition of something memorable causes the déjà vu, as though a wire in the memory circuit has been activated.

Human sacrifice has been practiced all over the world. Almost always, without exception, it is begun and administered by the priestcraft and religious rulers. It is the perfect example of entire peoples and religions going over to the dark side.

E.T

ONE NIGHT I had a long dream in which a teacher was telling me that I, along with several million other Earthlings, was an extra-terrestrial: an E.T. According to the instructor, there were many Souls on Earth with specific missions, very large and important missions that in many cases people were entirely unaware of; others were aware.

At night many of these Souls were leaving their physical body and were engaged in all manner of helpful activities for other Souls, and the planet. Others were proficient at helping the Force while still in the body during the day, and many advanced extra-terrestrials, those who remained outside of their physical body permanently, were continuously working not only on the Physical Plane, but on Earth's Astral, Causal, and Mental Planes as well. Planets have higher "bodies" as well.

According to this teacher, there was a general consensus among the planet workforce that big things were happening on Earth, that there was a special dispensation occurring. These E.T.'s were from all over Creation, and only a few seemed to consider Earth their home planet. The appellation E.T. seemed to come up time and again during this part of the dream, and upon awaking the next morning, the letters E.T. were bouncing around my consciousness like an over-listened-to song one can't get rid of. The dream then shifted sharply.

In the second part of the dream, which directly reinforced the first part of the dream, a friend and I used a rocket ship to visit my home star on the Astral Plane, located in the constellation Como Berenices. A handful of old friends turned out to greet us at the landing dock. It was home sweet home. The dream was very short with little detail and ended as we were back on the spaceship, searching a four-dimensional hologram for a "wormhole" that would take us back to Earth.

I was up early the next morning after these dreams, as I had a long drive to Los Angeles from where I was spending time in Sonoma, California, six hundred kilometers to the north. The two dreams were still fresh and vivid in my mind, and once on the road I reflected on them as I drove along while the radio quietly played music in the background.

I was wondering what the advantages would be of knowing one was an E.T. just as a march on the radio was finishing up. It was the Olympic theme song, the *Rondeau from Sinfonie de Fanfares,* by Jean-Joseph Mouret. The radio announcer named the song and composer, and then in a much louder voice, shouted out the spelling of the composer's last name at twice the volume the music had been playing: "MO–my initials–U R...E T! It was like a slap in the face. It came out as though he were talking directly to me with perfect prosody and inflection: M O, you are E.T. I couldn't help but laugh at such incredible synchronicity, and of course, it completely reinforced the dreams from the previous night.

I was still shaking my head an hour later when I stopped for gas at one of the "pit stops" between Los Angeles and San Francisco. As I got out of the car, a large sign, high up and partially obscured by a building in front of it, stared me in the face with large letters: MARK. My curiosity aroused, I moved slightly to the side as to be able to see the rest of the lettering. There were two more letters: ET.

Comments: It may be helpful to define just what an extraterrestrial is, since from one definition, everyone is. There is good evidence that the current human race on Earth did not originate here and that humanity on Earth evolved under similar conditions elsewhere. The "missing link" had not yet been evolved on Earth before the arrival of modern humanity.

Furthermore, is one talking about Soul or body? Perhaps neither the Souls on Earth or their bodies are from "here." However, it may be said that generally, most Souls on Earth have been temporary residents, reincarnating on this planet continuously for a very long time. The E.T.'s have not, and are here for various reasons related to their individual missions.

As the dream related, there is something special happening on Earth, and the evidence is everywhere: an increase in the democratization of the globe; the increased recognition of women's rights; the burgeoning sensitivity to animal rights; the widening umbrella of individual rights; the explosion of differing paths to realization; the planetary unification due to computers and communicative devices; the incredible discovery of new technology; the continued prevention of nuclear war; the spread of educational resources; the exploration of space…. Additionally, each religion is expecting their Savior's next incarnation, and many paths are expecting an ensuing miniature Golden Age or millennium.

Naturally, this must all be balanced, and the resulting juxtaposition of increased consciousness versus violence and natural disasters is striking. Some are seeing the demise of Earth, while others are heralding the beginning of a new Golden Age. And if the uptick in development is true, who is responsible?

Higher Souls who have incarnated from varying levels are responsible. If the destiny of Earth were left to its normal residents, Earth would still be in the Stone Age. It is the E.T.'s as channels for the Holy Power who have propelled Earth into its future, and every field of endeavor on Earth has been affected by their presence.

Many of the Souls so described know something is going on or suspect it without being able to articulate what is happening. Some feel as though they are awaiting orders; others are already conscious of how they are participating.

There is much tension and curiosity among these individuals, as many are waiting for something definitive to happen that would further define their place in the Sun. Many of these Souls are very experienced at what they do and have been on missions that last for millions of lifetimes; even so, current updates on exactly what the Holy Spirit is up to are hard to come by, and even the highest Souls are often given information on a need to know basis. However, the Hand of God has increasingly shown Its cards, and parts of the plan can be deduced by observing the wonderful effects occurring on the planet today.

Frequently, the effects of a Spiritual surge are difficult to discern, because they are not the effects people expect or desire. For instance, there is always much talk about peace; the Holy Spirit does not care about peace on Earth. There is also much talk about wiping out poverty and disease; the Holy Spirit does not care about that.

God cares about Soul, and the "education" of Soul's consciousness: this means the gloves are off, even during a "Golden Period," and the experiences necessary to instruct the globe's consciousness will be provided; it is the growth in awareness and consciousness that makes an age golden.

An additional reason for much current uncertainty is that few E.T.'s are physically conscious of what wonderful works they may be engaged in while their body rests comfortably during the night. 99.99 percent of all Spiritual work done by Soul is unknown and unavailable to Its own physical consciousness.

The human consciousness is like the old-fashioned fuse box: a little too much juice and the fuses overheat and blow; for the physical consciousness, that can be disastrous and cause a lengthy setback. Soul protects Its physical consciousness like a mother protects her baby.

It has been said that everything is a conspiracy: this is true, and the Holy Power is at the bottom of the ultimate conspiracy. This dream gave a glimpse of part of that conspiracy and further identified some of the co-conspirators.

THE FOLLOWING EXPERIENCE was short and poignant, as most Spiritual happenings are. I was sleeping deeply when I suddenly had the awareness that I had returned from the Lord knows where and was about to reenter the body. I surveyed the surrounding environment, which was a beautiful pastoral landscape. I was in everything; I was everything. I was the sky, the wind, the air and the earth. I was in the animals, insects and birds; I was the insects, animals and birds. I was the Universal Presence, silently watching and waiting; there was nothing I was not. I focused on a frog sitting by a pond: I was that frog, the ground it was sitting on, and the pond it was by.

Comments: Chuang-tzu is considered one of the founders, along with Lao Tzu, of *Taoism*, and he is famous, among other things, for describing a dream he had as a butterfly. As the butterfly, he forgot he was Chuang-tzu, and upon awaking, was not sure whether he was a butterfly dreaming it was Chuang-tzu, or Chuang-tzu having had a dream he was a butterfly. Perhaps he was both and more.

The Holy Spirit is everywhere and is everything. When one has an experience of being one with the "Force," they will be everywhere and everything. It is astounding but true; God's Body becomes Soul's Body. Soul becomes omnipresent, omniscient at Its level, and concerning the levels below it, omnipotent.

This experience usually happens on the fifth plane of heaven and represents becoming one with the Holy Spirit; it occurs as an adjunct to complete Self-Realization, a process begun at the beginning of the fourth plane, when the human Soul sees Its own Self for the first time, and glimpses Its own glory. At this level, the top of the fifth plane, Soul cannot tell the difference between Itself and the Spirit of God.

There are major differences between becoming identified with the consciousness of the fifth plane, versus the mental enlightenment experienced on the third and fourth levels of heaven, where Soul becomes one with the dual forces of the mind. Ironically, being the Spirit of God accentuates individuality, and unlike enlightenment, those attaining it never belong or remain within a religious tradition; religion and Self-Realization are antithetical to each other, and as Carl Jung, the co-founder of modern psychology stated: "Religion is the last defense against a Spiritual experience."

Religions, philosophies, and the enlightenment they aspire to are of the lower worlds; Self-Realization and the realization that one is Spirit are of the higher worlds. The former glorifies mind; the latter glorifies Soul and the Holy Spirit. The better way to God is to realize that one Is–for starters–the Higher Self, and enlightenment of one's mind will automatically occur without concentrating on it as a goal.

Flying Fun

ONE NIGHT WHILE fast asleep, not long after the previous experience, I became conscious of flying in space with twelve fellow Souls, all arranged in a perfect circle and traveling at an incredible speed. The bodies we were inside of were transparent forms or presences that somehow had a thin degree of corporality, or perhaps it was just my imagination. The twelve of us were returning to our home planet from a nighttime mission on another sphere, and we were high to the point of giddiness, having just been used to affect some wonderful development that had saved many.

Just what had occurred I was not thinking about in the dream, and as we zoomed along, members of the circle began exchanging places with the Soul opposite them on the circle's circumference. As they exchanged positions, they would enact graceful acrobatic moves, performing summersaults, pliés and the like in stunning counterpoint harmony.

One of the Souls present was my stepdaughter on Earth and as one of the ballet-like exchanges brought me next to her in the circle, I whispered telepathically into her "ear": "Wasn't that an incredibly beautiful experience?" We shared a moment of incomparable bliss! Of ourselves, we had done nothing; the Holy Force had done it all through us, and we were grateful to be used as channels.

Subsequently, we began entering our home planet's atmosphere and gradually decelerated. As we got closer to the surface of the planet we began passing puffy, white cumulus clouds that had beautiful, miniature, Camelot-like cities nestled within them. They were of three different florescent colors, red, blue and green, and they contained castles, tall minarets and buttressed palaces.

Suddenly, the habitations we were descending to appeared below, a small village comprised of several skyscrapers that were incredibly tall, hundreds of stories high, and spaced roughly a kilometer apart. There was thick tropical vegetation everywhere on the ground, and while I did not give the height of the skyscrapers any attention, I was semi-conscious of some underlying reason they were so tall, perhaps even two or three kilometers high.

Our Soul circle came to a perfectly soft landing at the base of one of the skyscrapers and immediately separated into different directions, dispersing like a "petaled" flower suddenly opening and losing its petals to the wind.

My daughter and I zoomed up to the 130th floor of the nearby building, entering through a window into our apartment. My wife, the same Soul I was wed to on Earth, was just getting up, engaged in a full stretch. Two bodies, presumably my daughter's and mine, lay on beds in back of her.

Comments: This experience was just plain fun, but it also brought up worthwhile information to contemplate. Of course, the main thrill was being used by the Force to help and serve God's cause, which includes everything. Those serving God enjoy the joys of channeling; there is nothing to compare it to.

The beauty of this happening was so intense that I cannot quantify it, and the feelings felt were so deep and ecstatic. How can one describe such?

The sheer loveliness of the cloud cities haunted my imagination for good, and the feeling of camaraderie with the group of Souls involved was magical. Everyone was perfectly on the same page.

It was also an insight into my Self being in other realities, along with my wife and daughter. It was a completely separate existence on another planet, but the three of us were identical to our "Selves" on Earth, even though the particulars of our relationship were different.

Atman, as an extension of the Divine Self, has the power to incarnate pieces of Its consciousness into vehicles all over Creation. The number depends on the evolvement of the Soul in question and Its mission. The possible numbers are staggering for an advanced Soul, while Souls beginning their Physical Plane incarnations struggle to deal with one unit.

Worthwhile

ONE MORNING I awoke repeating a phrase over and over again, perhaps five times in a row, before waking enough to become conscious of what I was doing and stop. The phrase was simple enough: "Nothing down here– Earth– is worth thinking about."

Comments: Thoughts are things, have existence, and are made up of elementals. They have a vibration rate: "good" thoughts have a high vibration rate, "bad" thoughts …. Thoughts of a relatively consistent vibration rate polarize one to the corresponding plane of existence with that same vibration rate. This has everything to do with where one ends up after this lifetime on Earth, and what kind of attitudes and temperament one has while on Earth this lifetime.

Naturally, if one wishes to attain higher planes, one must think accordingly, and imbibe those states of consciousness that match those high worlds. Unless one wishes to reincarnate on the physical plane, one would wish to transcend this world's consciousness and its concerns.

Most worldly business is incredibly simple and requires only minimal attention; one's thoughts can be on the higher life. Even those worldly duties requiring more focus can be approached with a Spiritualized attention that is contemplation in action, or, one may stop thought and simply watch their Self in action.

Of course, this is incredibly difficult as one's mind and emotions are constantly assailed by all manner of negativity, which on this plane is much stronger than the positive. This takes mental discipline, which means thinking what one wishes to think. The mind is simply a computer, and while reprogramming it may take time, it is not that difficult as one can use its proclivity to habitual responses to one's advantage.

The key to success at this rests with daily Spiritual "sessions": these not only help Spiritualize the consciousness, but open one up to the Holy Word which will come in and do all the work; it will only seem like one is doing it.

Paths

ONE NIGHT I dreamed that I was preparing to go to an inter-galactic seminar that would feature presentations on differing and various Spiritual paths. As part of my preparation, I was contemplating which paths I should bring to the seminar, choosing out of several hundred displayed on a very large wall. A one-meter fishing line with four evenly spaced fishhooks attached represented each Spiritual path, and as I deliberated in front of the wall, I wanted to take only the cream of the crop to the seminar.

I began taking special favorites down from the wall and very carefully laying the one-meter lengths in a large round barrel that I had procured for storing them. I had so many favorites, and I could not resist deciding on more and more of these wonderful ways of looking at the Creation and how to attain realization.

Suddenly, I noticed that the barrel was almost full, and it hit me that all of the hooks and lines were so intertwined that it would be impossible to sort it all out: a *Gordian* knot if ever there was one. I became very frustrated and irritated.

The dream then switched to the site of the seminar, and millions of followers had shown up to defend their "way." So contentious had things become that the authorities were staging fights between champions representing the various groups, and the first two fighters, escorted by huge crowds of fanatics, were moving towards an elevated boxing ring.

Unable to restrain their anger at competing believers, opposing sides began viciously fighting and dead bodies lay everywhere. So intense was the fighting that the authorities decided to call it round one, even though the fighters hadn't even reached the ring. In the next scene of the dream, I found myself in the pressroom with other reporters and photographers who were there to cover the main event. I had a large camera that I was very familiar with, as I had used the same model on Earth. As I prepared to take some photographs, I grabbed a flash attachment, and in attempting to attach it to the camera, ran into a bit of difficulty, but after a couple of attempts I slammed it into place.

Comments: This archetypal dream neatly summarized some basic principles concerning Spiritual paths, the first being that there are countless methods for approaching the Divine. They are all intertwined and come from the same place: the universal religious consciousness. Differences are due to semantics and the fact that they originate under different cultural conditions. Since the big religions are mainly from the Astral Plane, their main focus and worship is of sex and family, whether they realize this or not.

These paths usually have "bait" and "hooks" to snag their prey, each bait and hook appealing to a different body of man: Physical; Astral; Causal; High Mental. Bait may be the promised healing potential converts are looking for, social interaction, eternal security, or emotional fulfillment through the aforementioned sex and family.

There will be an intellectual component with plenty to chew on for the thinkers, and of course there will be guaranteed rewards for all after death of the body. Most people do not get into religion for pure and positive reasons, like say, the love of God. They have a long list of desires they are hoping to realize and are ready to defend their list to the death; of course the priestcraft take advantage of this, and as the Christ within Jesus said, the religious leaders are twice cursed, being in the ditch themselves and leading others into it.

How ironic that religious followers are fighting and killing each other by the millions. The original teachings of the major religions are pure and truthful but have been gutted by silly arguments and misguided, crystallized interpretations. The great Tibetan Lama, Rebazar Tarzs, neatly summed up the main characteristics of religions: superstitious assumptions; ritualistic ceremonies; emotional extravaganzas; metaphysical speculation; and ethical principles. No wonder not one Soul has ever attained Self-Realization or full Salvation through a religion; it is impossible to do so through their methods.

One is never going to realize God in church or by following a list of do's and don't's. And telling God that one is a believer is a nice start, but the various saviors cannot transfer the consciousness needed to their devotees that would allow these followers to establish themselves in a high heaven. Consciousness must be earned via experience and realization. If it could be given, God would simply give it to Soul.

Until one goes inside their own body, they will not find what they are really seeking: realization of the Self. They already are what they are seeking, but they have not realized it yet, and when they do, they will stop seeking. They will realize that they are Soul and were all along; one cannot be anything else; however, one may mistakenly identify as, or with, something that is not Soul, such as the body, the emotions, or the mind.

To be clear: one has a Soul, in the sense that one has a Higher Self; in addition, one IS Soul, even in the human body.

The last scene of the dream had the final answer, as the last scene in problem-solving dreams usually does; the true path is the "flash," the Light from the Higher Self and the "Holy Force" that illuminates everything and anything that one wishes to "picture." There is no other true path.

Visit to Alakh

ONE EVENING I dreamed of visiting *Alakh Lok*, the first positive plane of the higher worlds. This is the sixth plane of heaven, according to the system being used here; it is absolutely without negativity, pain, suffering, or death; its residents are immortal. This is the beginning of the mythical Garden of Eden.

At the beginning of the dream, I opened a book to its first page, which read: "Welcome to Alakh Lok." Without that beginning to the dream, I would not have known what the dream was about. Since the consciousness of a visit by the Higher Self to this region could never be transferred to the human brain, whose senses only work with Earthly stimuli, the Higher Self is forced to use metaphors and symbols to communicate with the human consciousness. A human being would face exactly the same problem if attempting to communicate aspects of human life through a dream to a sleeping ant.

In the second scene of the experience, I found myself in the basement of a gorgeous six-story house. It was shaped like Saint Andrew's cross, or a plus sign in math, and situated in a tropical landscape, with verdant greenery and copses of palm trees randomly placed.

The dwelling overlooked a beautiful sand beach that welcomed a turquoise-blue sea, and the vibes felt as though it were the Golden Age: perfect peace and bliss.

As I was there to do some temporary work on the house, I had been given a small room on the bottom floor, and after stowing some gear, I set out to explore. The first thing that simply jumped out at one was that there was absolutely no dust of any kind anywhere. There was a crystal-clear clarity to all objects that I had never experienced before; it went beyond clean.

I noticed three statues near an entryway that were carved out of jewels. They represented two monks protecting a young child and appeared to be sculpted from emerald, ruby and sapphire. Again, as I studied the statues, the lucid cleanliness of them, and everything else, smacked one in the eyes.

I proceeded up a floor and entered a simply furnished lounge area. I was barely into the room when two couples, formally attired and sitting on a large couch, sprang to their feet like lounging troops springing to attention when an officer enters the room.

"Can we help you? Is there anything you need?" several exclaimed at once. They all looked intently at me with such sincerity that I felt slightly embarrassed.

"Uh no, uh I was looking for a friend," I fibbed, not sure if I was supposed to be wandering around there.

"Oh, can we help?" they chorused together. "What does he look like, and where might he have gone?" They were instantly mobilized, and so eager to be of assistance that it was overwhelming. They wanted to help so badly!

"Oh no, ah, it's okay," I stammered, "I'm sure I'll bump into him around here; it's not important at all, but thank you so much." I hurried from the room.

As I proceeded down a hallway, I passed by what appeared to be a large orchestra room. It was mainly dark with chairs and large instruments silhouetted against dim shadows. To one side was a grand piano with a light over the music holder. A man and woman were sitting on the bench, completely absorbed over a musical score, too engrossed to notice me passing by.

In the next scene I was on the top floor at the back of the house, and I opened a door to a little balcony that abutted the house. As I placed a foot onto the balcony, I noticed that the wood was rotten and old: it looked ready to detach and fall if I ventured onto it any further. I hastily stepped back. It would have been a long fall. The balcony's condition was in complete contrast to the rest of the house.

In the last part of the dream, I was on that beautiful beach, and there were people of all ages spread about, enjoying the beautiful sunshine while sparkling blue waves crashed and crept up the soft-sand slope. However, I noticed that while everyone looked as though they were contentedly enjoying themselves, they were all busy doing something simultaneously: one older gentleman with gray hair was intently studying what appeared to be a manuscript as he reclined in the sand; a woman was explaining something to a pair of children while drawing complex equations in the sand with a reed; several children closer to the water were building incredibly complex sand-castle "cities," with incredible architecture and a system of canals that funneled the wave water throughout, powering all manner of little boats and crafts they had fashioned out of shells; others, sunning themselves in lounge chairs, were reading books, or engrossed in working little devices that I was unfamiliar with. Everyone was busy with something yet seemed to be relaxed and happy.

Comments: There is a peace that is unexplainable on the sixth plane of heaven that makes the Self feel so good that one can feel it in their physical body on Earth: one of the many reasons for this is that when one discards the Soul Body, becoming the Spirit-Self, a desire for experience and manifestation in the worlds below is gone. It is a little like getting out of jail, forever, or getting rid of a long-standing annoyance. One is truly free.

This plane is positive for the first time, and everything about it dwarfs into insignificance the regions below, be it size, the number and happiness of its residents, the brightness and intensity of the light, or the purity of its beauty. It is never destroyed and so infused with joy and love are its inhabitants, that there is little motivation to move on; Souls and Spirits are ecstatic.

Every Soul here is engaged on a mission they have chosen, and they are eager to help God's cause any way they can, not because they have to, or have been assigned a job, but because they deeply desire to. The compassion for others and the urge to help is so strong here that it could embarrass one, making them feel like a Spiritual flake.

Most of the Souls and Spirits living here have united masculine and feminine energies, the two sides coming together on the fifth plane. Neither the feminine Soul nor masculine Soul lose any of their personal individuality but fuse into something greater that was existent previous to being separated for the sojourn below. As Soul evolves, becoming an individualized part of something greater is constantly occurring; after all, we are all part of one Being yet always remain distinctly singular.

Many Souls here have missions that involve contributing to the Holy Spirit or Sound Current, symbolized by the dream's two musicians in the orchestra room. Uncountable Souls here play their part in channeling the Holy Spirit into the worlds here and below. The light and sound passing through these entities makes the stars on the Physical Plane look like mere fireflies on a dusky night. Everything in Creation is "run"; it doesn't just happen.

It is perfectly possible to fall from this region, as the decrepit balcony in the dream pointed out: one does not want to backtrack on what they have become; falls are disastrous, causing the affected Soul to lose gains that have accumulated over a long period of experience.

There are many categories of Souls present in Alakh Lok. There are those who are progressively descending (involution) and have not experienced the lower dual worlds yet; there are those who have evolved to this plane, entirely finished with their schooling below.

Some are recent arrivals (children), and others have been here beyond time. Most have continued as united between what was formerly masculine and feminine; others are singular and lone wolves.

In addition, there are large numbers of visitors who are working on establishing themselves here permanently. There are relatively few present here who currently have bodies on the Physical Plane. Those Souls here with bodies in the lower dual worlds, work on staying out of those bodies permanently, and run them from this plane or higher. They must master this before moving on.

Creation on this plane, and the ones within, is live-wire. There is nothing here that is not being created and maintained on the spot by Souls residing here, including the entire plane. Form has seriously faded here, although not entirely gone, and instead there is increasing perception, light and sound.

This plane is often subdivided into two or three planes, and while Souls and Spirits here are very evolved compared to those below, they are naïve and inexperienced in the higher worlds compared to those further along. They often attempt missions that are impossible to realize, due to their lack of perspective. The next dimension, *Agam Lok*, will address that.

While Souls residing in Alakh Lok have tremendous powers, such a one would never know it from the human consciousness' viewpoint. Every gain by Soul is met with change, challenge, and death in the human consciousness, which is discovering its own "wrongness" and vulnerability.

It can seem as though the work on the lower self is barely begun. Every gain in consciousness and perception in the physical consciousness, passed down from within, uncovers deeper layers of false identity and hidden desire; one's Spiritual progress is matched by a deepening realization of their own human "darkness"; naturally, this "darkness" must be addressed.

Serpents

ONE NIGHT I dreamed of facing a very large king cobra, considered the most intelligent serpent of them all. I was in a rather enclosed room that was semi-dark, and the cobra bit me four times: twice in the left hand, once in the left calf, and once in the right hand when I grabbed him with both hands and crushed his skull into mush.

I looked at my hands. An icky tar-black filth bubbled out of the large holes where the snake's huge fangs had punctured the flesh. It continued for ten seconds or so, and then the wounds closed up as though nothing had happened.

Comments: This is one of many dreams in which I encountered the serpent kingdom; they were always venomous, and I was bitten almost every time. However, as scary as these dreams could be, they were wonderful Spiritual communications.

The venomous serpent is the perfect symbol of the Holy Spirit, and being bit in a dream simply points to an infusion of Spiritual consciousness. The Eastern half of the globe understands this; the Western half, naturally, has an opposite interpretation: Satan. It is quite understandable that they would arrive at this conclusion: they are "of the world" and the Holy Spirit to them is venom; they want nothing to do with this fiery energy and are fearful that their carnal desires will be compromised. They are prescient.

When one is initiated to some degree, they are infused with more consciousness, and their vibration rate is increased. This begins a new rebalancing, the old having to adjust and conform or perish, the new taking its place. This is not always easy or pleasant as old habits, attitudes, and practices get modified or dropped; some may be ripped away.

Having the increased Spiritual consciousness (venom) injected into my unconscious (left hand, left calf), mashing its head, and getting bit again in the process (right hand, conscious of), symbolizes the mastering of the received awareness. When one dreams of killing the snake, stepping on it, or handling it as a friend, it means that the recipient is incorporating what was given.

In the oldest Greek myths, Hercules' first labor was the killing of a giant serpent, and he lost his right index finger in doing so. While still in the cradle, he also strangled two large vipers that had been sent to kill him.

The Christ within Jesus compared Moses' lifting up the serpent in the wilderness to His own lifting up, and of course, *Quetzalcoatl,* the Savior of Central America, who the Mormons believe is an earlier incarnation of the Christ, is the Feathered Serpent. In the Eastern half of the globe, the serpent is often worshipped as a symbol of the Divine, and its lore is ubiquitous.

Little Johnny

LITTLE JOHNNY IS four years of age, and he is a normal red-blooded boy with the energy of three adults. His family is just about to move into a new cabin that uses a wood stove for cooking and heating, and since the burners are always hot, Johnny's parents have worked for several weeks preparing him to be careful around the stove.

They lectured him several times, explaining in detail what would happen if he touched the red-hot metal. His father took him by the local fire department and cajoled one of the firemen to say a few words on the dangers of fire. Grandma showed Johnny graphic pictures of burn victims, even going so far as to have Grandpa roll up his pants leg and display a horrible scar received when Grandma accidentally knocked him into the stove. Johnny's mother was especially protective and made sure he was listening to her warnings by questioning him several times about what she had said.

By the time Johnny's family moved into the cabin, they had inculcated an impressive amount of knowledge into their son on the stove's dangers, bearing in mind his age. He could give the temperature of fire, the difference between first, second, and third degree burns, and even draw a picture of what a terrible burn looked like, modeled after Grandpa's leg.

Johnny has knowledge. Question: Is Johnny going to touch the stove?

Comments: Of course he will. Johnny has knowledge and information, but he is without realization and wisdom; wisdom will begin when he experiences first touching the stove and realizes–real eyes–that it is indeed hot. Realizations translate into wisdom that become Spiritual consciousness.

Johnny's parents, his grandparents, and the fireman could not give him this wisdom. It is not that their attempts to were a total waste; knowledge is the beginning of wisdom and prepares the way for understanding experience.

This is exactly the Spiritual predicament humankind is in today: they worship intelligence as though it equates to Spiritual wisdom; it is the other way around. Until totally retrained, the mind is the enemy of Soul, and its so-called intelligence obscures rather than illuminates the truth. Why?

Soul's wishes are anathema to mind and its agenda. On this planet, the more intelligence, the bigger the ego, and some of these intellectuals start believing they are wise. They are little Johnnys that haven't touched any stoves; in other words, they have not experienced God.

This is why there are not any shortcuts to God. Many seekers believe that there are secrets which, if they only knew, would not only give them special powers, but also elevate them into mastership, sainthood, or some other lofty goal. There are secrets, wonderful secrets, but none that can evolve Soul one iota of growth. That comes from experience, and much of it, as few learn quickly. The experiences produce realizations, and deep realizations become Soul's very consciousness, a work that has been in progress forever.

This is also why high agents of God cannot bestow the riches of heaven on their followers, or anyone else. However, they can do tremendous things that assist aspirants getting these riches for themselves. Many argue that it is impossible to succeed Spiritually without the help, support and love of those who have evolved to the higher levels. Others like to keep their distance. Both are, at differing times, perfectly okay, as individuality, freedom, and self-determination are prized by the Spiritual Forces.

Guru Nanak, in the *Jap Ji*, writes: "Let he who thinks he has the power try"; this will definitely uncover one's total powerlessness and need for assistance; might it be from one's own Self?

This begs the question: Spiritually, what is the best way to touch the stove? If one does the Spiritual exercises daily, very gradually expanding them into a permanent point of view, one will find that they have become, at some level, a virtual God-stove, warming others as a channel for the Holy Fire, while seeing their own impurities gradually burning away.

Upside Down Cake

ONE NIGHT I dreamed that I was face to face with my father. He took an angel-food cake, with thick chocolate frosting and dumped it upside down over my head. I was enraged. I screamed at him, "You're telling me to get lost!" Several months later, I again confronted my father in a dream and hit him in the face as hard as I could several times. It felt really good!

A year after that, I dreamed that I was "white-hot" regarding my father. I rented a convertible, drove to the center of town, took the top down, sat on the top of the back seat, and opened fire with a high-powered rifle at totally innocent people. After shooting several persons, I drove to the police station and turned myself in. I said to the Desk Sergeant, "I totally lost it!" I was sick with remorse.

Interspersed with these dreams, and well before and after these dreams, there were other dreams that featured a total loss of control due to this anger: driving a car at night and the lights fail, or the brake pedal goes to the floor. In one dream I lost the brakes, lights and steering wheel while speeding at night. I pulled the emergency brake: nothing. I shifted the car into reverse: nothing!

These dream experiences were occurring after forty years of being on the "path" and attempting to follow truth. Anger was still coming out, as major energies were still unwinding the psychological engrams of youth, and past lifetimes.

The big problems have many tentacles emanating from a scarred center; the tentacles represent the symptoms and manifestations of the core issue and the feelings that were created. These feelings, revisited in dreams, are at the heart of the challenge, and provide a clear picture of what needs addressing.

The emotions involved are often overwhelming, because as one releases the energy of a serious problem, they seemingly go through it all over again. It can seem the height of irony. Of course, dreams are about the dreamer's perception of what happened and may or may not be based on objective truth. My father has his own version, and we had long since been very close. The victim card does not work in the game of self-healing.

One must see and take responsibility for their part in creating monster problems and understand and forgive the part that others may have played. Anger is overwhelmingly self-pity that compounds and perpetuates earned karma. Nobody else is responsible for one's problems but them.

This author, fool that he is, believes there is no real way for an aspirant to be successful at solving their core problems unless through daily Spiritual devotion, they open themselves up to the power of their Higher Self, and by extension, the Holy Power of God. Besides the best counseling possible, this will power the new direction, making it possible to succeed, where as attempting major change without this Divine assistance, even with the best psychiatrists in the world, will fail.

The Master Therapist is inside one, and if one can discern and follow Its guidance, they will gradually and progressively be healed, step by step, of every affliction in each and every "body."

The Music of the Universe

ONE MORNING, JUST before waking, I heard the most beautiful music imaginable: the sound involved is indescribable, but I can describe something of how It was created.

Everything in Creation has a note, a sound, and usually many sounds that are resulting from the Force flowing through them. At the center of one's Self is a deafening, euphonic waterfall of sound with thousands of frequencies streaming out to perform various functions, audibly heard like "…the sound of many waters."

In this particular experience, every single thing in Creation was joining in a glorious symphony by playing their notes and holding them for differing lengths of time, which created the most beguiling syncopation. It was so enchanting, so harmonic, so gleeful, such a paean to joy and overflowing happiness, that It pulled at one to join in with one's own sounds. It was truly a universal orchestra with all invited to join.

Comments: There are many reports and stories of hearing this music, usually by those that make a practice of "going within," but also by musicians, composers, and singers. When comparing listeners' descriptions of their experience, it becomes apparent that there are many ways of hearing this Music of God; however, all who experience It are totally enthralled!

This Music, which is actually the Force or Word in action, creates and is reflected in all the audible sounds of Creation, be it in the music that people love and listen to or the sounds of nature's sonatas. Every sound, be it the roar of ocean waves, or a style of music, carries a field of consciousness with it made up of thoughts, feelings and points of view native to that band of consciousness. The song the mockingbird listens to, is the song it sings.

Beethoven reportedly heard this music and attempted to imitate it in his ninth symphony: the fact he was stone-deaf made no difference as this Music is heard from within.

A Visit by Agam Purusha

ONE NIGHT WHILE sleeping I became aware of walking down a forest path, located near my hometown, but on the Astral Plane above (within) Earth. As I slowly sauntered along, I literally gaped at the lush beauty about me. The towering trees were brightly adorned with jeweled leaves and huge pastel blossoms, their branches growing into and merging with other trees; beautiful birdsong and harmonic whistling echoed through the glades; little ponds were everywhere with brightly plumed water birds swimming about; fragrant flowers flowed in chains from tall stately stalks that wound round the trees like holiday lights.

Out of the corners of my eyes I could see gnomes, fairies, elves, sylphs and the like darting about, but if one looked directly at them, they were too shy to be seen outright, and would quickly leap out of sight. They were astoundingly graceful and beautiful, a beauty on Earth only seen in young children.

Suddenly, there was an earth-shaking thunderclap that ripped the sky open overhead, sounding like a giant wood match being struck along a rough surface, and so loud that the ground shook-shuddered. A split-second later, a beautiful brown-skinned young woman with long dark hair and dressed like an Amazon warrior, stepped out from behind a large tree a short distance to my right. With her eyes and a little tilt of her head, she directed my attention to her right.

There, thirty meters to her right, was a stunning sight, a crazy-white ball of light, crackling and buzzing while hovering a meter above the ground. It looked like a radioactive basketball-sized sun of immense power as it hummed and vibrated, sending out power waves that seemed to set the entire landscape undulating as though we were on a floating dock in windy waters. I was reminded of ball lightning, something I had witnessed as a youngster in Minnesota during a thunderstorm.

It was obvious now that this powerful ball of light, bursting into this dimension, had caused that ear-bursting explosion that sounded like thunder, and I stood gaping at it in stupefied awe.

Before I could react, strong rippling winds that were circling the Light-Ball shot out straight at me and encircled me so tightly that I could not breathe. Then, unable to move even a muscle, I was propelled straight up into the air as though shot out of a cannon, perhaps one hundred meters above the ground.

Looking down I said to myself, "If whatever this Power is drops me, I'm going to splat like a bug!" As soon as I said that, even though it was silently to myself, I shot up much higher, perhaps a kilometer above the Earth.

Well, I thought, if this Force can control me like that, It should be able to ensure I'm not dropped, and there's nothing I can do about it anyway. I resigned myself to this Power.

I was still unable to move although I could now breathe. Abruptly, with a quick motion, the Force holding me bent me into a reclining position, as though I were sitting in a lounge chair on some beach, and we started slowly sailing sideways through sky and clouds towards a lake that nestled against the city below. I had no freedom of movement and was literally along for the ride. There was absolutely no communication with this Being, and it handled me the way one might handle a sack of garbage.

It was seemingly a beautiful summer day, and the ride became serene and worry-free. As I cruised out over the lake, my reverie was suddenly interrupted as I was forced into a gradual descent towards the lake's edge far below. Judging the angle of descent, it looked as though I were going to be gently set down on the beach, but about one hundred meters from the lakeshore, while still fifteen meters above the lake, the Power unceremoniously dumped me into the water as though I weren't worth the trouble of carrying a meter further.

I could sense the disdain in the gesture, perhaps even contempt. I felt for and held on to my wallet that was, naturally, soaked with the rest of me, and I swam to shallower depths, stood up, and slogged towards shore. I felt so excitedly good.

I crossed a road that abutted the beach and entered a small restaurant, but some of the customers had seen me come in over the lake, and they gave me strange, uncomfortable looks that bespoke fear. I decided to go home. I could not believe what had just happened but was giddy and wanted to tell someone.

When I arrived home my wife and four-year-old daughter met me, and I exclaimed to them: "You'll never believe what just happened to me!"

"Tell me tell me tell me, I wanna hear!" my daughter shouted while jumping around like an excited monkey.

My wife, who appeared very calm and bemused, said to her with a smile, "Calm down and let him tell you."

Comments: This experience was a real barnburner, with a dramatic intensity that shocked one with its realness, a reality that penetrated one more deeply than ordinary sensory experience, accompanied by a plethora of wild emotions. I confess that if I had not read and heard about similar experiences that other believers had gone through, and if I had not read of what this aspect of one's Self is like, I would have been clueless, and needed more information from inner sources (if cooperative) to interpret what had happened.

However, this Force that accosted me in the dream is well-known and inhabits the dimension above Alakh Lok, both inside one's Self, and of course, the same hierarchal position in Creation: called *Agam Purusha* in various Eastern teachings, IT is said to represent the Power of God.

This dimension is the ultimate wake-up call and makes all below paler than pale in comparison. It is often equated with the beginning of Divine wisdom, whereas, below is merely Divine information and Divine knowledge. It is as though one has entered the Marines after a soft spoiled childhood, and Agam Purusha is the drill sergeant.

So severe is the adjustment that many fail to establish a "home" here and retreat to the happiness and joy of the positive gradations below. What is it that makes this dimension so difficult to fathom and integrate?

The use of power is one obstacle, but the big one is the realization of eternity, and that affects everything. It is as though the Power of God is going to show one what is really going on behind the scenes. Of course, it is staggering.

Just before the dimension Agam Purusha rules, Souls have been enjoying the use of their creative powers in the first positive levels of heaven, and these powers are impressive indeed. Of course they are used for Spiritual purposes, as these Souls are evolved and free of the lower worlds.

Nonetheless, they have been directing Spiritual powers from their own personal point of view to a degree not possible on Agam Lok, as on this higher plane all discretion has been turned over to the Divine Self; one is totally along for the ride, a slave to one's Essence, as Saint Paul so eloquently elucidated in the *Christian Bible*.

True power comes from peace and stillness and the surrender of its use to the Divine Self. Souls in Agam Lok have further realized this through missions on Alakh Lok that, quite frankly, failed, relative to what a particular Soul or Spirit had hoped to accomplish. Why? Perhaps it is Spiritual naiveté. There is no hurry in the heaven worlds, and living the future is further exposed as insanity.

There is a well-known Indian axiom that is considered absolute truth; "The mill of God grinds slowly and exceedingly fine." This concept is exponentially expanded on Agam Lok to the unimaginable and unfathomable. There are no numbers that cover eternity as God is without a beginning, and the time, in Earth terms, for advances in Soul's station are so daunting that future goals become merely academic; it is as though one has been told that for their next advancement, they are to chop down every tree on Earth with an axe; where does one wish to begin? and how quickly does one wish to go?

This contrasts with the promises made by teachers who claim that they can shortcut this process, ushering their chelas out of the lower worlds in one or two lifetimes, or maybe, in hard cases, three or four.

The Christ within Jesus addressed this: "And no man hath ascended up to heaven, but he that came down from heaven, even the Son of man which is in heaven." Just the experience (time) needed, if known, to transition into a new dimension for the first time, and then establish oneself, would discourage almost all aspirants. Why?

They are living the future. They have set future goals, Spiritual goals, and staked their happiness on reaching these goals, thinking a future "now" will somehow be better than the present one. It is true that a future achievement might find one in a better position, but that could be an eternity away. What about now? Maybe one should relax a little: maybe a lot. Even in a hypothetical better future, one is going to have to live that "now."

Soul only has the present moment, and all in Agam Lok is live-wire creation every moment; there is no past or future. Consequently, Soul, in establishing Itself here, attempts to remain here continuously, whether It has bodies in the dual universes or not.

Agam Purusha compels one to live right now, and forget future achievement; ironically, this enhances further realization.

The "relaxation effect" encountered here affects everything, as one realizes there is no way to speed eternity, whether it is in helping other Souls or changing one's Self. It is difficult to impact Souls that have lived forever; anything that could be done quickly would have already been done. Helping other Souls is somewhat like helping a mountain: it's best to take the long view.

Souls on Agam Lok increasingly realize that they can perform any task, simply because they are letting God's power within do it all. Can a water sprinkler take credit for watering the lawn? It is easy to be confident when God is backing one up and doing everything.

The Sound is much greater than the Light in this region, even though the Light is beyond description. Sometimes on Earth, weather events reflect light conditions from this dimension, albeit much lessened. Falling snow in ambient light, or hard rains with the Sun out can remind one of Agam Lok's light storms.

Some Souls get lost in these storms and are not sure where they are. However, Soul's GPS is the Sound Current, and one familiar with its variations in different dimensions can determine their location. Generally, the further one goes in, the higher these sounds become. For this reason, when listening to the Sound, it is considered best to concentrate on the highest frequency one can discern.

A further aspect of this experience worth mentioning is that it was the anima figure, represented by the "Amazonian" woman, who directed my attention to this Power. This is consistent with the work of Carl Jung, Maria Von Franz, and other psychiatrists who feel it is the feminine consciousness within man that not only knows where the truth can be found, but can direct one to it, while acting as a guide, mediator, and channel. My daughter and wife, at the end of the dream, probably represented my anima at the time (daughter) and what it was to become (wife). Ironically, it was my daughter that many years later pointed this out.

There is little communication with this aspect of God and Self, and the Power aspect of the Almighty can appear very cold and heartless. The destruction of whole galaxies that contain billions of life-bearing planets can shock the human emotions, let alone the wipeout of entire planes of Creation. Power and love can seem antithetical to each other but in reality are two sides of the same coin; power not only makes love possible but is also the foundation for all life; without it, nothing would even exist.

    Since the Absolute is without form, cannot be seen, and at the Center cannot be heard, one is left defining God as this Power. This Divine Power IS, and to be controlled by this Power is Soul's deepest desire; under the Divine Self's control, one feels like a baby loon, safely ensconced on its mother's back lest a pike grab it from below.

Incomplete Bridge

ONE EVENING, NOT long after the preceding experience, I dreamed of driving over the "Grapevine," seventy kilometers of mountainous freeway north of Los Angeles that cuts through the San Gabriel Mountains. I decided to get off the freeway, and I took the next exit ramp available which started ascending in a wide spiral that quickly began carrying me to dizzying heights. Looking ahead, I observed that the ramp abruptly ended in mid-air where it was still under construction, and that it would eventually bridge the distance between two peaks a kilometer or so apart.

I stopped the car a short distance from the ramp's edge and walked to the area under construction which consisted of concrete forms and crisscrossed layers of rebar. I nervously got down on my hands and knees and very gingerly crawled towards the very edge. I cautiously looked over the last concrete form: it was a very long way down.

Comments: To accept one's Spiritual inheritance is a heady business. One's Spiritual destiny is so glorious that it makes accepting it in the human consciousness difficult. Each step taken must be digested and made one's own, and the Spiritual sojourn is full of big steps. It is not long before one feels "way out there," completely separated from one's normal life and, oftentimes, the people in it.

Accepting Soul's progress is easier if one sees it as a present reality rather than something to be accomplished. After all, one is the Divine Self; one does not have to create It, or become It: one simply has to realize that one is It through direct experience.

The ugly duckling did not have to become a swan,
it had to realize that it was a swan.

Anima

THE ANIMA, AS used here, refers to the feminine principle in man, and of course its opposite, the animus, refers to the masculine principle in woman. A Spiritual seeker will be faced with understanding and integrating these principles into their overall consciousness; there is no way around this. For those who desire clarity on this subject, the works of Carl Jung, Maria Von Franz, and their associates are recommended. They are invaluable in understanding the unconscious and have been pioneers in dream interpretation. Since there is much good information on the anima available, I will be brief.

This poor fool was raised in a male family where physical and psychic violence were an everyday occurrence. There was little room for the anima to express itself, and it was effectively isolated. Emotional displays and the feminine viewpoint were seen as weaknesses and held in contempt. Proving one was "tough" was a primary paradigm.

As a result, my first encounters with the anima in dreams were not pleasant; "she" hated my guts and was seriously out to "kill" me. "She" would show up in dreams as a beautiful woman dressed in black as a witch, right down to the conical hat. "She" was wily and fast and schemed to get her revenge on me for past treatment. "She" was very angry!

The resulting personality behavior, which reflected this "death demon," was negative, critical, and devaluing: etcetera squared.

As the years passed, things became better. Dreams began showing the anima frozen, tied down, or covered up, and the messaging could not be ignored. One very complex dream pointed out that my father and his ways had effectively "killed" the anima within me.

Increases in awareness, provided by difficult experiences, taught the beauty and importance of the feminine viewpoint. In addition, Spiritual women in my life were invaluable in providing insights into the feminine perspective, and books such as *The Dance of the Dissident Daughter,* by Sue Monk Kidd, helped to understand Souls in female bodies. My relationship with "her" began turning around.

After another decade or two, the anima's presence in dreams became positive, and "her" place at the council table became more important; "she" constantly channeled understanding, forgiveness and compassion; "she" was also encourager-in-chief, and several times I literally heard "her" say things that were so positive and affirming that I was somewhat embarrassed. I wish I could say that I did a good job following such guidance, but I failed much more than I succeeded: much more, and still am.

After another decade, I had three or more experiences indicating some degree of union with this personification of the unconscious. In one dream, I kissed this beautiful woman, and it was a kiss like none other ever experienced on Earth. Two other dreams took on an even more intimate tone; however, I will omit details lest they be misinterpreted, but they connoted union with this element.

I must note here that this is a continuing challenge, and I claim no expertise on the subject: quite the reverse. However, in my little world, compared to how things initially were, there was much improvement.

Women I have shared Spiritual notes with have reported similar challenges in unshackling their animus; however, in giving supposed insights on that subject, I would feel like a dog talking about cats. I'm totally unqualified. The aforementioned literature, in this author's questionable opinion, is invaluable if one seeks understanding in this area.

One final clarification: one does not follow their anima per se but follows what this feminine consciousness is channeling and facilitating: communication with the Higher Self.

The anima's personal perspective is at the "council table," along with the other members of one's personal constitution, and given due consideration as befits its status and position.

The Grand Ball

THIS DREAM-LIKE EXPERIENCE one evening, after falling asleep during devotions, which is a common occurrence, had a clarity and realness that routinely forces its way back into my day-to-day stream of consciousness.

In the first scene of this experience, I was a servant dressing to attend a formal ball, and I was highly anticipatory; this was to be a huge event. I finished dressing and entered the main ballroom, parking myself unobtrusively to the side, watching for instructions from the host of this event.

The guests were just arriving, and more regal and beautiful couples have seldom been seen. The men were all in uniform: they looked to be in their thirties and of all races. They exuded competence and confidence.

On their uniforms, much like soldiers on Earth, their chests were full of little rectangular ribbons that symbolized medals awarded for various missions and service. When one looked closely at an individual ribbon, it would emit a series of light images to the viewer that told the story of how such award was won. The missions for which the medals had been awarded were incredible. They lasted hundreds of trillions of years and involved whole cycles of galaxies, universes, and planes. These individuals were masters of some august level.

The ladies accompanying the men wore lovely floor-length gowns in white or pastel colors; they were beautiful, confident women who were elegantly coiffed, and they surveyed the room with studied awareness; they missed nothing. It was clearly evident that each couple were really "one," so to speak, as something about the way they were together spoke of total trust, closeness, and understanding. I understood that the awards symbolized on the men's uniforms were for the couple together. These couples could not have been more impressive!

The host of this gathering was greeting couples over to my left, and he was dressed in white toga-like apparel rather than a uniform. He was wearing just one ribbon of a turquoise color near his neck. I knew that he had a drawer full of them as I was responsible for overseeing his quarters, but I had never seen him wear any but the one he had on tonight and that only one other time.

It amused me to see that the guests could not keep their eyes off of this turquoise ribbon, and if they furtively snuck a long enough glance, they received some of its "tale to tell": their reactions varied from stunned to awed, and although the guests were discreet with their curiosity, they resembled Cub Scouts secretly eyeing a Marine General's uniform. Some were caught staring and flushed deeply.

As evolved as these guests obviously were, the host was quite apparently from a higher dimension, and it fostered a little bit of uneasiness in the room. I laughed: while in the host's presence I had never dared look directly at the ribbon and had no idea of the story behind it. I just didn't dare look.

The host was all graciousness as he met each of the attendees. He smiled effusively and expressed a keen interest in each guest, yet questioned each couple together regarding the histories on the man's uniform. He appeared to be a paradox in that he was totally relaxed and gentle, laughing and joking, yet everything about him breathed incredible power, like a set bear trap ready to be sprung. He played dumb like there was nothing unusual going on, but nobody believed it.

There was tremendous tension in the room. These couples had been summoned here, and they did not know why. I noticed some concern occasionally on some of the faces; these Souls were not used to being in the dark as to what was happening, and so far, the host wasn't talking.

After greetings and introductions were over, the guests continued talking with each other, and the room was filled with animated discussions and laughter. There was little for me to do, as there was nothing to be served. It was understood that the host was to address the group later in the evening. My primary job, organizing these meetings, was mostly over.

While closely watching the host lest he nod instructions, I saw him adroitly slip out of the room through a hidden door behind floor-length drapes. I knew he was headed to his office for a quick check, as I had seen him visit this particular room regularly as though the work in there needed semi-continuous attention. The host never mentioned anything about what he did, but I had seen into the room once as he came out the door. One whole wall was covered with computers that had wavy lines on the screens as though something were being monitored.

I inconspicuously slipped out of the ballroom as well in case I was needed, but he was already coming out of his office, evidently satisfied all was well. Before he noticed me, I saw him pause and go into some kind of love-thrill, lifting his arms with eyes closed and silently emitting joy for several seconds.

I pretended I hadn't noticed, as he passed by me with a smile and quietly slipped back into the main room. It was all so quick and inconspicuous that I don't believe the guests noticed his absence.

Comments: This dream built on the "E.T." encounters I had experienced years earlier and offered fascinating additions to what was already known. Not only were Souls being gathered for some tremendous mission on Earth, they were from extremely high places. The fact that these guests showed up in pairs illustrates that they were from the positive God-Planes and were not from the lower dual worlds; they were complete units.

The ribbons on the men's uniforms also denoted missions that circumscribed lower world cycles in time and space, and one might guess that they represented Souls working for Alakh Purusha, or some other higher plane authority. Every Soul is working for someone.

Apparently the host was from a place higher yet, and the turquoise ribbon represented a mission at a higher level than these couples were used to dealing with. To have Souls on Earth from the higher planes is a rare occurrence, as Souls on large Spiritual missions are most often from the third and fourth planes of the dual worlds. If true that there are Souls here from high above, one may expect momentous effects on Earth. This group's consciousness will impregnate Earth's consciousness, and every creature will be reborn to some degree. Perhaps this is occurring right now.

If one wishes to judge or discern whether there is a nascent Spiritual increase on the planet Earth, do not look for peace or the end of violence; rather, look for an increase in awareness; Earth will always have a balance of positive and negative.

The fact that high Souls attending the ball had no knowledge of what was going on is a recurring motif in Spiritual experiences. No one seems to know what is going on and those that do know aren't talking. However, if one is given a tidbit here and there, either through inner experiences or contemplation, it is not that difficult to surmise the big picture, although the objective details seem to remain hidden.

One more point: these high beings are God-lovers.

Pinned Down

ONE NIGHT I dreamed that I was to introduce a speaker from a famous monastery to a large auditorium of guests. The speaker, unnamed in the dream, had an excellent Spiritual reputation, and the guests were anxious to hear him speak. As I sat waiting on the stage, I noticed that there were various dignitaries present. Some wore robes denoting various religious orders and others appeared to be clergymen. Most looked like everyday people although a few carried what appeared to be scriptures.

The moment arrived and I stumbled through brief introductory remarks that I do not remember. The speaker, who was an imposing figure dressed in a black robe with a cowl, reminded me of the emperor in *Star Wars*.

Before speaking, he slowly sauntered down the center aisle, staring intently from one side to the other, all the way to the back of the auditorium. The cowl he was wearing forced him to turn his head further to the side than would normally be required, making his perusal more personal.

His back now to the stage, he slowly turned around, as though in deep thought, and carefully walked back to the front, repeating his close examination of the audience. The crowd's anticipation was palpable. One girl near the back giggled but was quickly silenced.

Subsequently, he stood behind the lectern and solemnly scanned the crowd. Without saying a word he projected total confidence and authority. He began speaking in a loud commanding voice: "I have examined the auras of every Soul in this audience, and there is not one individual here that is more evolved than the second level of heaven."

The audience was stunned. There was a shocked silence and painful disbelief, and then in unison, as though a choir rising to sing, they ran for the exits as though someone had yelled, "fire!" There was pushing and shoving in their hurry to leave. It was but a few moments, and the auditorium was entirely cleared.

The speaker looked at me with a quizzical look and the palms of his hands up as though to say, "What did I do?"

Comments: There is a hierarchy in Creation, and, like it or not, every Soul is somewhere on "Jacob's ladder." Naturally, like everyone else, Spiritual seekers may fall prey to getting ahead of themselves, imagining that they are further along than is true. Many aspirants, especially in men's bodies, imagine they are avatars, saints, masters, reincarnated saviors, prophets, and the like. Others claim Self-Realization, God-Realization and other exalted states. Many fantasize that they are the "chosen one."

These dreams, usually false, are the fruit of the ego, which should be awarded the "Distinguished Cross for Service" noting its exemplary work. The lowest person on Earth often believes they are "King of the World." People could not cope if knowing their true station in Creation; the reality of their situation in eternity would overwhelm them. Enter the ego.

Of course, this is part of God's plan, and Souls progress by imagining themselves as better than they are, and then attempting, and eventually succeeding, in matching the imagined state with their thoughts and actions. It's a Spiritual "Catch 22": if one wants to imagine and believe that they are at a particular level, they will have to act accordingly. One has to see it in their life to believe it.

Some teachings preach that one must kill the ego. This is incorrect thinking. First of all, the mind and ego, even if they could, would never kill themselves. Is the fox that is guarding the henhouse going to go hungry?

It is true that Soul administers terribly hard reality checks to the ego that feel like deaths, as one's identity gradually switches from mind to Soul, but the ego recovers and takes its rightful place at one's council table. This process, when completed to a satisfactory degree, allows one to pull back their ego whenever necessary, much as one pulls back their emotions when required. One has realized who they really are, Soul, and who they really aren't, mind and ego. The ego is now a passenger in the back seat, its driver's license revoked.

This concept of the ego is called *ahamkara* in Hinduism, the "I maker," and is responsible for our individuality and self-awareness in the human body. It is part of the mind element on the fourth plane, often called the Buddhic or mental plane. Others call this *Par Brahm*, the Bliss Plane, or *Daswan Dwar*.

When one says, "I think that blah blah blah…," this is the ego expressing itself. Put simply, there are two levels to this principle. The first is the gross ego, the rather obvious ego that most levelheaded people are aware of, and secondly, a rather "subtle ego" associated with the unconscious level at the top of the fourth plane (*Saguna Brahm*). The first is rather obvious; the second is not.

The problem for the Spiritual seeker, and it is a major problem, is that Soul (before realizing Itself) identifies with the ego; unrealized Souls believe they are the ego, their "I-ness" on Earth, and not Soul, a completely separate consciousness. The Spiritual separation of the two is a complex painful process; many feel (at times) that they have been killed in action. One's false identifications go down swinging.

The ego separates one's interests from other people's interests. This is good, not bad, as it is easy to see how this grows individuality, one of the Creator's main goals. God does not want cloned conformists passively following outer authorities. The system is designed to create and nurture unique individuals that rely on nothing but their own inner authority. Once the ego and mind understand that they are sergeants, and not the General, they are invaluable in assisting Soul in Its Earthly mission.

The mind and ego are so close to Soul that at times it can be difficult to separate them. So close are they that one feels no differently out of the body, minus the ego, as when in the body, with the ego. Perhaps a main difference is that when minus the ego, one has lost their concern for Self and experiences a heightened concern for others.

The speaker in the dream did not give his audience a "back door," an escape avenue for their dreams and goals, fantasies though they may have been. He cornered their egos, destroying their chance to believe they were something greater than they actually were at that time. Perhaps he needed a lesson in compassion and understanding.

The Appearance

ONE AUTUMN, WHILE visiting a favorite contemplation spot in the San Gabriel foothills, I decided to landscape the immediate area. The place I sat overlooked a three-meter waterfall in a narrow canyon, now dry, that when active dropped the water onto a pile of rock and sand about two meters high.

I decided a pool at the bottom for the water to splash into would be an ideal touch, and I began excavating the mound at the bottom, removing rocks and sand with a shovel. This was quite obviously insane right from the beginning, and it turned into a Herculean task as some of the rocks were huge and had to be pushed, shoved, and rolled out of the way. I became obsessed. Afternoons after work I would spend a couple of hours digging, and after three months, and dozens of visits, I had finished a three-meter diameter pool about one meter deep. If I could accurately share the amount of work and energy I put into this project, it would not be believed.

There was still some time before the expected arrival of the rainy season, and I decided an overlook, high up on the canyon's side, would be a nice finishing touch. There was a little flat ridge the size of a small room twenty meters above the waterfall that was perfect, and I spent three weeks removing chaparral and leveling it.

Everything was now ready, and all that was needed was enough rain to start the canyon stream flowing. I couldn't wait. December eighteenth, three days before Winter Solstice, it began to rain, and over the next two days enough fell to get the canyon streams flowing. The following day, on a beautiful sunny afternoon, I hiked up to the spot, my imagination running wild.

The scene was perfect, resembling a postcard from Hawaii: the stream was flowing nicely; water was splashing noisily into a filled pool, and birds were loudly singing and bathing at the pool's edge. While climbing up to the observation perch, I could not stop smiling. The surroundings were like a Zen garden.

I began contemplating a dream from the night before in which I was moving with my Higher Self into a new apartment. "He" was taking the front room near the door, while I was moving into the room at the back of the apartment.

Abruptly, I was jerked back to my physical surroundings, as I noticed a large ball of funny-white light slowly bouncing and bounding up the canyon floor. It was very distinctive: it appeared as a perfect circle about four to five meters in diameter, edged by a very clear dotted line of alternate dots and dashes, which also alternated between black and white. Its movements were purposeful yet effortless, and while it resembled nothing on Earth, it was clearly conscious. It radiated a presence.

It seemed free of any earthly restraint, floating over the waterfall and continuing its ascent up the narrow canyon, disappearing from sight. The observation porch had provided a perfect view of the incident, all fifteen seconds. I was dumbfounded; I had no idea.

I sat in a trance for minutes attempting to make sense of what I had seen. My mind was a total blank, ironically just the state needed to pick up some clue or flash of understanding, but nothing was coming. Subliminally, I slowly began to become aware that there was a commotion on the opposite side of the canyon, perhaps forty meters away, but I didn't want to lose my inner place, so to speak, and focus on what it was. However, the ruckus became so disruptive that I had to look.

The opposite side of the canyon from where I was sitting was a vertical rock face, easily one hundred meters high and one hundred meters across. There appeared to be a chipmunk dashing around its surface like a crazed demon.

I have a history with chipmunks and am familiar with their capabilities, but this was beyond belief. He would cover thirty meters in one literal second, faster than ninety kilometers per hour. In addition, going straight up the rock face at a ninety-degree angle slowed him not a bit. He would dash from one side to the other, then straight up for fifty meters, then down again at full speed and keep right on going into the next variation. This went on continuously for fifteen minutes!

It finally became obvious to me that I was being told something about what I had seen. As soon as I realized that, the chipmunk vanished from my sight.

Comments: This experience, and others that happened simultaneously, occurred five years and ten months after meeting Agam Purusha and dealt with the top of the same dimension. It is impossible to describe such a place as it is the very top of manifest Creation, and Light and Sound, which have just manifested from within even higher regions, are at their peak. Being in the center of a nuclear explosion would be a nothing comparatively.

Of course, a human consciousness cannot experience it, but it does experience the effects of one's Essence traveling there. There are many names for this region: some paths call this *Anami Lok* and its ruler *Lord Anami*, the Nameless One.

The chipmunk metaphorically represented my own "chip off the Monk," my Atman, Higher Self, or whatever name one wishes to call this intermediate consciousness between the Human Soul and Divine Self. It was demonstrating Its total freedom from my body It had permanently vacated, now running it from a distance, or different dimension. It, like the chipmunk, was totally free. Of course, this manifestation was scaled down lest I be burned alive, as Soul's Body is far greater than any star.

It is important to revisit the fact that this journey is occurring within one's own bodies; the Human Soul climbs Its own hierarchy, merging and blending with each "station" of Itself as it progresses.

It is true that as one explores these levels of consciousness within oneself, they will simultaneously explore the "outer" macrocosm that corresponds to said level. However, the Lords of the Planes encountered are within one's own Self and are one's own Higher Selves.

A strange merging occurs at this point which is hard to articulate, but it feels as though one has become the Self that one formerly looked to for guidance and data. There is a human limitation on this as one cannot encompass such an "Ocean," but one is at least swimming in It, and in a real way it feels like the two have become one.

I was making this very point to my wife one dark night in the foothills above the Los Angeles area, as I was pacing a short distance back and forth in the place we were sitting. Exactly as I finished making the point, a terrifically large rattle erupted right at the base of my feet; a large rattlesnake had slithered up unseen in the darkness to participate in our devotions, and I had walked right into it. Thankfully, it did not bite me. I took the rattling as a confirmation of made point.

It is incredible the level of awareness the human consciousness can "pick up" and receive from the Higher Selves. It is worth noting that this has nothing to do with intelligence or a higher degree of thinking ability but has everything to do with increased perception, awareness, and knowingness. These are not created or developed by the human consciousness but are given to one by Soul.

Simultaneously, in the human consciousness, a thick layer of illusion is laid bare, further exposing unconscious, automatic reactions to external challenges. This usually focuses on family and one's early conditioning and those Souls that have had a tremendous influence on one for good or bad.

One at this point usually has moved past following any particular person's wishes or commands directed towards one, but they may find that they are reacting to them nonetheless, perhaps doing the opposite or such, simply because of the emotion involved. Oftentimes, one has unwisely made a fetish of their independence.

This is a trap. Why? It may cause one to act against one's Higher Self's interests and directions. Actions based on reactions to something or someone could be termed a "reverse curse"; it blocks accurate communication with the Higher Self in affected areas and can have devastating consequences.

The ideal presented at this level is that one should be ready and able to follow the Divine Self at all times and in all things. Like other abstract qualities, this is always a matter of degree; there is always room for further growth and expansion.

Of course, landscaping in a canyon is worse than stupid, and further rains destroyed all traces of my landscaping adventure.

Neanderthal

ONE NIGHT SHORTLY after the previous experience, I dreamed I was driving my car down the highway. Sitting in the back seat, on the passenger side, was a large Neanderthal man, dressed as one might expect.

I slowed the car and pulled over to the side of the road. I calmly got out of the car, walked around to the other side and with a smile, opened the back door, motioning for the Neanderthal to get out and sit on the passenger's side front seat.

He was so happy: he couldn't speak but made raspy-grunting sounds of excitement while pressing my hand. He looked at me with tearful eyes of joy, as he climbed into the front seat. I got back in the driver's side and drove on.

Comments: This dream brought back childhood memories of sibling disagreements and such to determine who could sit "up front." It was a big deal. What Soul wouldn't want a closer view of the action?

It was amusing to be pictured as a Neanderthal: it reminded me of Agam Purusha's tangible contempt for Its own lower component: me. I was being allowed in the front seat, but there wasn't going to be any driving. This involves closely watching what transpires without being the initiator.

The Chinese Tao, or "way," has a concept describing this state called *wu wei wu*: it means to do without doing, or active inaction. It is a difficult state to describe, because when one is "in the flow," it "seems" as though one is actively participating in making it happen, but the bottom line is that one is not doing a thing. The Divine Driver is doing it all, even the little physical and mental minutia that one thinks they are doing.

Bee Nice

IT HAD BEEN a long stressful week, and I was aching to get away from people and take a long walk in nature.
    I drove up to the foothills bordering the town I lived in and picked a canyon walk that was popular with many on the weekends. However, it was mid-week and I hoped for a people-less stroll in quiet solitude. Aldous Huxley once said: "The chief beauty of nature was the absence of man": I could not agree more.

As I began sauntering up the road, things began to go south almost immediately. A car pulled up and parked just ahead of me: five children, two dogs and a loud man with more words than time to say them piled out of the car, apparently ready to head in the same direction I was. I was horror-struck. I sat down to consider my options.

Thankfully, the children holding the leashes could not quite restrain the dogs, and the whole cacophonous clan was dragged up the road and out of sight in minutes. I waited a little longer and then continued walking, pretending nothing at all had happened.

Abruptly, a car's alarm began sounding, and although some distance away, it echoed loudly through the canyon. The car's owner was probably hiking and away from the car, as the alarm just kept going and going.

I swallowed the annoyance and kept walking, but I had hardly begun when a runner in back of me, holding a loud transistor radio in one hand, began slowly gaining on me. He would run forward for a bit, then run in place for a bit, the result being he stayed close behind for several minutes. When he finally passed with a friendly hello, I couldn't even look at him.

Other hikers coming from the other direction passed me. I looked the opposite way entirely as though they were diseased and contagious. I didn't even want to look in their direction.

Things were just quieting down when the first group I'd encountered began coming back towards me from the other direction, louder than ever as one of the dogs had broken free and taken off up a side canyon. I wished I'd brought my earplugs.

I sat down by the side of the road, turned my back to the noise, and waited. Twenty minutes later all was finally quiet, and I continued walking, but had barely gone ten meters when the runner with the radio came into sight from the opposite direction. He waved and smiled as he passed; I said nothing and stared straight ahead.

By this time I had gone as far as desired, and before turning back I decided to sit for a spell under an inviting sycamore tree, carpeted with long green grass underneath. It was momentarily quiet, and I needed a respite from what seemed like constant annoyance.

As I sat down in the grass a large hornet stung me in the left ear, and before I could stand back up, five more stung me in the face: I had sat down on a hornet's nest in the grass, and a large swarm of bees had gone airborne. I ran. One more stung me directly on a large old scar I carried.

When I arrived home sometime later, it took me some time to dig out the stingers in my face (face them, Mark), especially one in the lobe of the left ear (better listen, Mark). The one in the scar (symbolizing this old problem) didn't come out for six months. It was very painful. After an episode such as this, one is not tempted to invite the next level of warning.

Comments: I knew the cause of this experience immediately. I was not acknowledging the Souls I passed along the way on my walk, and my Higher Selves were none too pleased. The meetings with these strangers were not incidental; they had been meticulously arranged, and my little space fetish had completely disrupted carefully planned objectives.

There are complex interactions between Souls in proximity that are seldom noticed or understood in the physical consciousness; 99.99 percent of all channeling is hidden, and the channel involved is completely unaware. Sometimes one may be graced with an insight or experience providing information that must be extended to the whole; seldom does one get extended glimpses of anything hidden.

Frequently, one may be interrupted during devotions simply because they are in the desired state to be an effective channel for God. Ideally, one should not mind the intrusion; sometimes it is an opportunity to give. The Christ within Jesus said to His disciples: "You have been freely given to; now freely give." It is a truism that Soul survives by giving.

Souls on this planet are not self-contained: they desperately need acknowledgement, confirmation, attention, respect, and "love" from others. Those who have reached Spiritual adulthood do not "need" these things from people, as God has provided them with infinitely more than any human being could ever offer.

These "adults" are in the perfect position to vitalize others, not because of their social skills, although those may be of use, but because Soul, when desired, can impregnate any interchange they participate in with tremendous energies. The physical consciousness is not in control of this, other than being open to it.

A little innocuous comment made by a channel, when empowered by Soul, may change some individual's life forever; or, perhaps it may simply be eye contact that opens the window to Soul. Most often, the channel involved will know little of what may have transpired in higher dimensions, other than insight they may have gained from past-parallel experiences when the Holy Power lifted Its veil.

Left Luggage

ONE EVENING I dreamed that I was driving to a large airport for a scheduled flight. There was the normal tension associated with not wanting to miss it, and I felt hurried as I pulled into an airport parking lot that was some distance from the terminal. I began walking the kilometer to the terminal at a relaxed pace; I had plenty of time.

I entered the terminal and checked the flight board; everything was fine. I took a seat and opened a magazine.

Suddenly with a start I realized I'd left my luggage, two large suitcases, in the trunk of the car. How could I forget it? I looked at the time and realized I could not go back to the car for the luggage and still make the flight. I would have to leave it behind.

The last image of the dream was of this huge airliner ascending at an impossible angle, nearly straight up.

Comments: This short dream included three symbols of karma: the suitcases (baggage), the trunk of the car (storage), and the car itself (body); all were left behind.

Perhaps there are some personal things in life that are not, in a manner of speaking, totally resolved. Perhaps there are some things that cannot be resolved. Many of these things must simply be left behind.

One leaves behind those things that qualify by removing one's attention from them: movin' on. One stops thinking or caring about them: forget about it. One relaxes about it: who cares? One releases it to the Force: let go, and let Soul.

The story of Lot's wife in the *Christian Old Testament* illustrates the consequences of being fastened to the past. She was warned by an angel not to look back but disobeyed and was metaphorically turned into a pillar of salt; her life became paralyzed, crystallized and frozen, bound to past events and unable to move forward.

Initiations

INITIATIONS IN LIFE are usually different than your common initiations in religious orders or social lodges; it is the Human Soul that is initiated. This literally raises one's vibratory level, and everything in the recipient's life is going to have to conform or perish.

Naturally, initiations are not bestowed lightly and are not conferred by those in the human consciousness; rather, they occur when the proper energies have been amassed, polarizing the aspirant to the desired goal. The only way to amass the energy needed is through a wildly insane love for the Divine, filled with thrills and joy.

There are thousands of initiations that are usually divided into loose groups or numbers, each number covering many steps and stages within its designation, and systems of initiations differ radically, beginning and ending in totally different places within evolution.

For instance, many systems begin with the person deciding to "go consciously with God's will for their life," while others may start at Self-Realization on the fifth plane of heaven. And conversely, some systems end in enlightenment on the fourth plane of heaven, or other such designated levels, while other systems go beyond the very top of manifested Creation. Naturally, systems do not match up too well and, as expected, followers of differing systems will have experiences according to their particular "map."

Common examples of initiatory systems are the twelve labors of Hercules, the adventures of Odysseus in the *Odyssey*, the fourteen Stations of the Cross in Christianity, the Ox Herding pictures in Zen Buddhism, or the Nine Stages of Tranquility in the Buddhist Mahamudra tradition. The Hindus, Sikhs and Jains have very elaborate and exhaustive initiation systems. Perhaps the first clarification needed when discussing initiations is the difference between unfoldment and growth, which are often used interchangeably.

Every Soul is an initiate in the school of God and occupies a position in the Spiritual hierarchy. They have progressed, or "grown" to a certain point in their evolution which is a relative constant that does not change very quickly through their countless incarnations.

"Unfoldment," on the other hand, as defined here, refers to a Human Soul's maturation in a single lifetime, as it reclaims the level of awareness that It has achieved through previous evolution. A highly evolved Soul who incarnates on Earth may appear to be growing rapidly but in actuality is simply unfolding into who they were before reincarnating: a high initiate. I would surmise that anyone reading this book is a higher initiate.

The term "unfoldment," is used broadly and often refers to the eternal unfolding of the Higher Selves as well, as they are unfolding their original glory.

The Holy Power has designed individual lesson plans for every Soul at that Soul's level, and these lessons, measured against the human Soul's incarnation length and karma, gradually bring Soul back to Its former level and position: if everything goes well. Anything beyond that would be considered an advance, or growth; anything short of what Soul had accomplished previously would be considered somewhat of a "fall."

Souls are not desirous of falling, and those evolved enough to be planning their own incarnations are careful to be born in circumstances conducive to their Spiritual success; many incarnate in groups so as to aid in each other's development. The planning for an incarnation in all circumstances is incredibly exhaustive by human standards; the stakes are high; any Soul at any level can fall. Note the myth of Lucifer, the Light Bringer.

Human Souls, high or low, do not skip any steps in the learning curve when incarnating: they start at the bottom and go through every step on their way back to their "home level." One may understand why high Souls must go through so much "life experience" and why a "beginner" may experience a fraction of that.

A highly evolved Soul may require thousands of times more experience in a single lifetime, as It may have to unfold all the way back to "graduate school"; perhaps the less evolved Soul only needs "kindergarten" experiences to attain their former station in evolution. Both in this example would be challenged to the full extent of their capabilities and undoubtedly take a "full" lifetime of experiences to reclaim their previously earned level of consciousness. It is hard to imagine what a Mary Magdalene, Buddha, Madame Blavatsky, Jesus, or other Divine Beings must have needed to experience to regain their consciousness.

There is a point worth interjecting at this juncture. Life on any plane anywhere is perfect and incredibly ordered. There is no chaos, other than in an individual Soul's life. There may be an appearance of disorder, but underneath all is perfectly in place and working exactly according to plan. One may ask: "How can this be"?

The answer: the Absolute has ITS "Body" under total control, every cell, and all is perfect, every now. What kind of Absolute God would it be if IT were not perfect? And how long would Creation exist?

Souls slide into the awakened life slowly, and lifetimes spent on the Astral and Lower Mental Plane involve being slowly shaken awake from the dream state. It takes much time to do this as the dreams of Earth prove false, and their existence as the nightmare of Soul is slowly revealed. Gradually, the consequences of foolish creations become unendurable. Bad karma is hell.

The third plane of heaven is often divided in two: the lower four sub-levels (of seven) are often called the lower Mental Plane;

the higher three sub-levels the Causal Plane. This is the plane Saint Paul mentions as visiting in the *Christian Bible*. It is at the beginning of the Causal Plane that the Human Soul wakes up, so to speak, and begins to see the big picture; It begins accessing and studying Its past incarnations and karma, consciously cooperating with Its own evolution. This is "old hat" to higher initiates, as they have been so engaged for a relative forever.

For the aspirant working "through" this plane, (going further), as well as the aspirant working "off of" this plane, (home base), several things are usually, if not always, taking place: the individual has made some progress in controlling the lower nature; they have made good progress in communicating with the Higher Self, or teacher, through dreams, visions, lessons, study, flashes, the Sound Current, and daily Spiritual devotions; their love nature has been electrified, vitalized, and directed towards their Higher Self or teacher; they can hear the Holy Sound Current within themselves, although they may not be aware of this; they are traveling at night out-of-body consciousness, although they may not fully understand this, or be aware of it; they are beginning to understand the difference between mind and Soul, and the difference between mental truth, and its antithesis, Soul truth; they are seeing through the gross ego and can usually pull it back when required; they are having experiences of various kinds which often center around problem solving; they will also be having various experiences with their Higher Self, although these experiences may be months, years, or decades apart.

However, Soul has not seen Its own Self yet. When Soul graduates to the fourth plane, often called the High Mental Plane or Par Braham, that changes in a most momentous way.

When Soul progresses to the fourth plane, It encounters a game-changing occurrence that completely dwarfs anything experienced previously: It meets Itself in Its own radiance and splendor. A more technical explanation would be that the Human Soul has stepped into the next dimension on the Astral Plane and met Its own Jiva, or intermediate consciousness between the human Soul and the Atman or Higher Self, face to face. Is It recognizable? The Christ within Jesus stated: "If you've seen the Son, you've seen the Father."

This is the resolution of the "mystery of the ages," as Saint Paul described it, and the secret guarded by millions of "paths." It is the beginning of Self-Realization, or true Salvation, and one is discovering their true identity. One's Divine Self (Christ Self) is manifesting as Jiva to the Human Soul.

In the *Christian Bible,* the Christ within Jesus eloquently expresses the promise of such a meeting: "The person who has My commands and keeps them is the one who [really] loves Me; and whoever [really] loves Me will be loved by My Father, and I [too] will love him and will show (reveal, manifest) Myself to him. [I will let Myself be clearly seen by him and make Myself real to him."] John 14:21 (*Amplified New Testament*)

So completely off the charts is this experience that it seriously unbalances all it occurs to. Frequently, the aspirant will believe they are the savior of a particular religion or if the person is secular, a famous incarnation, or some other divine personage. It may take a long time to understand that this is simply the signature event for all Souls establishing themselves on the fourth plane; one is not special in the way they may be thinking.

The fourth plane is often divided into seven sub-planes, each one so immense that one could believe each sub-plane to be the entire Creation. This plane deals with the higher mind and its ability to discern the truth. At the top of this plane lies what we term the unconscious, the last sub-level before the Higher Self or Atman.

Many paths such as Buddhism, for example, aim for this plane and the enlightenment it confers, hoping to ascend to the fifth plane (nirvana) from here. Sometimes the term "cosmic consciousness" is applied to this mental dimension; it is characterized by great feelings of happiness, unity, and oneness with all so deep that individuality may seem irrelevant.

One may have experiences of tremendous Light and will see God in everything. If the Soul involved belongs to a particular path or religion, they will usually remain within it, but their tradition will come to life with new meaning as never before.

Earth's greatest Souls, whatever the field, are from this plane and are the vanguard of the human race. Souls established on the "inner" side of this dimension are happy and enlightened, but they have not realized they are the Higher Self, let alone the Holy Spirit and the Divine Self.

It is in the *Chandogya Upanishad* that the saying, "that thou art," is first mentioned. A father is explaining to his son that one is Brahman, the All, or God. This short aphorism is put several ways and interpreted from several angles, but their meanings all coalesce: one is the Self they met in their signature experience, and it is time to identify with that Self as the vastly greater part of one's being. This is not so easy to do, as attested to by the extraordinarily great number of Souls here who are unable to complete that transition: they are often called "dwellers on the threshold."

Seth Dayal Singh, a respected teacher in the Sant Mat tradition of Northern India, claims that Souls on the fourth plane, which is still within the negative dual universes, cannot be told one thing: this is hard to dispute, and there are several reasons for this.

Souls on the fourth plane do not believe they are on the fourth plane of heaven; they believe they are God-Realized, have finished their journey and are at the top of Creation. It is much like a fourth grade student thinking that they have already completed college.

This is a common occurrence among Souls at several points in Creation and understandable as the planes reflect each other in ways that can make them seem similar. For instance, the great powers a Soul has on the fourth plane to marshal the negative forces and simulate creation, mimic and reflect true creation out of Spirit by a Soul in the positive God-Worlds.

In addition, Souls have lifetimes on the fourth plane reaching trillions of Earth years and, naturally, they believe they have attained the immortality conferred on the fifth plane and above. They are wrong, as the fourth plane will be wiped out after an incredibly long span, and Souls there will be put into dreamland until a new Creation allows them to resume their manifest existence.

The challenge Soul faces on the fourth plane is not to take meeting Its own radiant Self personally. But since the Viewer in this experience has not shed the Mental and Unconscious "sheaths," Soul on the fourth plane is still colored by the endless desires of the mind and unconscious to be someone important, a famous entity who deserves to be recognized.

This is the home of those baldly claiming to be masters, gurus, saints, avatars and the like. They are almost convinced that they are what they say they are, but a few million followers would help to believe it. Simply put, Souls on the fourth plane have not realized that they are Atman, but are still identified with the part viewing Atman, and it has gone "to their head." "Pride goeth before a fall."

Souls on the fourth plane are in process of "becoming" what they have "met" in the inner worlds. When the Human Soul has met Its own radiant Jiva, blending and uniting with It, It continues an ongoing process whereby as Jiva, it is striving to become united with Atman, or the Higher Self, which will occur on the fifth plane. This process is being repeated internally at all levels, as each component works to evolve into the next highest rung of one's own "Jacob's ladder."

Before Jiva can become one with Atman on the fifth plane, and complete the process of Self-Realization, a great death will occur, as ruling desires of the unconscious are crushed, and one realizes to a much greater degree that they are less than not important. Traversing this "dark night of Soul" is difficult, and many Souls, unknowingly full of themselves, spend countless lifetimes attempting to let go of mechanical, unconscious desires, and identify with Atman, which has little interest in the desires of the lower worlds.

The fourth plane is full of apparent contradictions: it is very evolved relative to the first plane in which Earth dwells, yet it is still in the negative dual worlds, and its inhabitants have not realized they are Soul; they unknowingly believe they are the mind. The goal of "enlightenment" is noble but a side direction. The goal, for starters, should be Self-Realization, or in Christian terms, Salvation. Just how enlightened can a mind be?

How does one work through the fourth plane? One forms an increasingly close relationship and communication with the Audible Sound Current within themselves and then follows Its guidance as best they can.

Locked In

ONE MORNING I awoke at 3:00 AM and arose to use the bathroom only to discover that I was locked inside the bedroom. I couldn't believe it! The door didn't even have a lock! Something had broken in the doorknob making it totally useless, and the knob simply spun around without engaging.

The door was solid wood and, as it opened towards me when functioning, this meant that while closed it was snugly against the door jam: attempting to force it with a shoulder or kick wasn't within my purview. I reached under it and pulled towards me, but it didn't budge a centimeter, and I could not find a thing in the room to attempt releasing the latch, which looked like a dubious solution anyway.

At this time I was staying on the second story of an apartment complex that was high off the ground floor. I did not have my phone in the room, and I hated the thought of yelling out the window for assistance; it would wake up so many people. What to do?

I sat on the bed and weighed my options. I decided that going out the window, perhaps with sheets tied together, was my best option. I sure didn't want to wait until morning to resolve this.

I looked in the closet, and my eyes went to three leather belts. I looped one of them around the rear leg of the bed that was close to the window, buckled the other two belts together with the first, popped the screen off the window, and hung the belts over the edge. I looked down below from the window. It was hard to tell in the darkness, but the "rope" looked three meters or so short: close enough.

I sat up on the window ledge and slowly lowered myself down hand-over-hand using the belts, straining my body to the limit.

When I came to the very end of the last belt, the tip of my toes just barely reached the ground. The "rope" length could not have been more perfect, and I hadn't disturbed a Soul.

I retrieved a hidden-outside key used for such emergencies and reentered the apartment. The bedroom door would not open from the outside either, and I had to take apart the handle to gain access to the bedroom.

This was crazy, and I needed to contemplate what my Higher Self was showing me.

Comments: Once one understands that dreams are metaphors they are much easier to interpret. There are also great books on dream interpretation, such as Sandra Thomson's *Cloud Nine, A Dreamer's Dictionary*, or phone apps like *Way of Dreams*, that can be very helpful. Of course, life on this plane is a dream and can be interpreted as such, especially unusual occurrences or experiences that stand out in some manner. This particular occasion of being locked in the bedroom is a prime example.

The bedroom in dreams often deals with intensely personal things such as sexuality and one's views towards it. I was "locked in" to something deep and unconscious here that I did not have a "handle" on, (inside or outside myself) and to "escape it," I needed a new viewpoint (window) that wasn't blocked (screen). The belts, perhaps, symbolized responsibility, since they are responsible for keeping one's pants up. I guess I was indebted for three times the normal amount. I needed the hidden key (solution) to reenter my locked apartment (problem in question), subsequently take apart the door handle (contemplate) and unlock the problem.

Problem solving experiences happen at the beginning of the work needed for resolution, not the end, and it wasn't long before this poor fool found out what my Higher Self was showing me.

The Heart of God

AT THE TOP of manifested Creation the Lights and Sounds are so intense that a description relying on one's imagination is useless. One might say it is like trillions of nuclear bombs going off every billionth of a second, or that the Light-Streams are like zillions of lasers multiplied a zillion-fold a few zillion times, but nothing would come close to describing this point in Creation of the Holy Spirit becoming manifest.

Just inside this point, vibration-wise, in the next dimension "in," all becomes totally silent and totally dark. Everything is present; nothing is manifest; nothing except your Self.

There is a dark void at the top of every dimension, but the Sound of the Force is always present with uniquely individual sounds that make that particular void identifiable. This void is without sound, and traversing the divide line between manifest and non-manifest Creation is going from insane intensity to indescribable perfect peace; it is wonderful. This is the beginning of many regions often called the Heart of God that appear to one as differing shades of black.

This is where one meets, merges, and becomes Paramatman, the Supreme Spirit, the Christ Self, the Divine Self, the Light Giver, or the Holy Spirit. Some describe this as Brahman or God which begs further definition: if one says they are God because they have identified as being a part of God's Spirit-Body that is understandable, but one is not a part of the Absolute or God in that sense. One is a part of the body or aura that the Absolute inhabits much as cells of one's physical body are distinct from the Soul inhabiting it. Some believe that the Absolute is even further removed than described here.

This is a very mysterious area that is difficult to describe, and there are also things here that cannot be mentioned and are best experienced. However, not everything is secret, and a few broad statements will not compromise proper Spiritual protocol.

One finds here that it is they, as the Divine Self, who is the Light Giver, and one will never experience Light as is present here, emanating from one's own Self; there is no other Light present. Staring into the Sun from a mile away would be child's play compared to the Light seen being generated. Guess whom your Divine Self looks like.

It is dangerous here, as the Human Soul is irradiated beyond what one can imagine, and one returns from this region glowing like a piece of steel pulled from a blast furnace.

The experience is so far-out exalted it can take years to assimilate and attempt to understand. It leaves one dazed, and pieces of the experience may surface to consciousness long after the initial happening, suddenly showing up as "a thief in the night." One's Higher Self sends additional communications elucidating aspects of the experience; this continues for years.

The point is strongly presented from several directions that one is Paramatman, Christ, or the Divine Self; one is also the Human Soul, Jiva, Atman, Spirit, and Light and Sound.

Strange, ambiguous images and aspects of the Divine Self are presented that boggle the mind and resist interpretation. Some appear in the negative, like undeveloped film. Other manifestations appear that cannot be described. The flow of the experience is surreal and like watching something from several viewpoints at once. All of one's consciousness "stations" are present and involved.

The Divine Self manifests two symbolic and highly important objects, one marking the present, the other foretelling the future. A sharp distinction is made between the lower and higher consciousnesses, the lower consciousness being the equivalent of solid concrete, the Divine Self being the Essence of the Holy Word.

A love is experienced that is beyond anything that could ever be said or thought in any language ever created, and one understands that they have been blessed with the ultimate in grace and mercy. All is dependent on this grace: all. There is no such thing as being worthy.

There is a signature event within the experience that is beyond communication. All who have been here know of it.

There are a small number of entities grouped together in the distant void that at first appear like stars but upon closer inspection reveal their identity.

One is their Divine Self; one is not.

Mountain Warning

ONE EVENING I dreamed I was floating down a peaceful river with my Higher Self beside me. It appeared as though we were encased in large transparent bubbles on top of the water, flowing "gently down the stream" along the base of a gigantic mountain whose sheer cliff-side rose straight up thousands of meters. The streaming Sun shone sweetly; the birds melodied, and all seemed glorified like the Golden Age of antiquity.

Suddenly, without warning, the entire mountain collapsed, coming down like a skyscraper after internal explosives have been detonated to destroy it. The resulting explosion blew me out of my protective "bubble" and halfway up a mountain on the opposite side of the valley. I landed on a large block of stone that was still wobbling from the gigantic blast, and I stood there rocking, completely disoriented.

It was so much like death that I fully expected to begin leaving the planet. My Higher Self, who had been beside me before the mountain's collapse, was nowhere to be seen.

Comments: After having this experience, I breathed a huge sigh of relief and said something to myself like: "Whew, glad that's over." I have jumped to that conclusion a number of times after unsettling dreams and have usually been wrong. This was a warning of what was to come.

Looking back I smile now, but I was far from amused at the time. Everything went south in the worst way for several years, and events played with my breaking point like wind playing with chimes.

One becomes thankful in hard times fully knowing things could be very much worse in a heartbeat. All Souls go to God for solace.

The Very Advanced Teachings

THE VERY ADVANCED teachings are very simple when it comes to describing what one might do to find God. Putting this "simplicity" into practice is another matter, somewhat like the difference between discussing how one walks a high wire versus doing it. Nonetheless, the "how to" is simple: establish a communication line with your Higher Self and follow Its guidance.

In order to be successful in communicating with the Higher Self, one will have to be committed to performing daily devotions, customized to the individual practitioner's needs and desires. These Spiritual exercises should over time, very, very gradually expand in the most relaxed sort of ways, not so much in the amount of time spent in them as in the amount of attention placed on a Spiritual perspective.

One should expect subtleties in their communications from their Higher Self: the "still small voice" seldom uses words although anything goes: dreams; visions; flashes; the Audible Sound within; signs; omens; internal voices; feelings; and much more.

In order to be successful in establishing daily Spiritual exercises, one will have to be self-disciplined and inspired: one's own mind will do everything in its power to prevent daily contact with the Higher Self from occurring. Simply follow the "otta law," and all will progress: do what one knows they "otta" (ought to).

I do not believe that anyone interested in God needs someone else to tell them what they ought to do. Those claiming ignorance in this respect do not want to do what they know they ought to do.

The above is all one has to do to contact God.

Here are some things that do not matter: it does not matter what position the body is in; paralyzed people have found God.

It does not matter if one studies scripture; God has saved zillions who could not read.

It does not matter how one breathes; the Holy Spirit has rescued people in iron lungs and on respirators.

It does not matter if one is blind, deaf, or dumb: "The Kingdom of Heaven is within."

It does not matter if one is in a religion, and as Carl Jung, the co-founder of modern psychiatry points out, religion is the last obstacle to having a genuine Spiritual experience.

It is known that there has never been one Soul saved through religion, as it is impossible. Why? Religious followers are looking for something outside in the back yard that is inside the house. They are looking outside themselves to saviors and scriptures for Salvation, whereas they must go inside themselves to meet their Lord. The greatest teachers in the history of Earth, and everywhere else, agree: "The Kingdom of Heaven is within." For those religious followers who have begun looking inside the house, it is just a matter of time before they meet the Owner.

It does not matter if Soul has incarnated into a female body; women have been told otherwise. They have been declared unclean, told where and where not they can pray, held unfit to be leaders, denied the right to serve in certain Spiritual capacities, mocked, undervalued, condescended to, patronized and debased. Certain Eastern religions believe that Soul in a feminine body cannot attain liberation. Need one point out how wrong this is. Who would do such things to women? It is usually male religious leaders, and they face the effects from their own actions in subsequent incarnations, usually in female bodies.

In actuality, there are strong advantages to incarnating into the feminine: to name just a few, a much stronger intuitive connection to Soul than man's; an unsurpassed capacity to love; frequent "deaths" to the ego due to societal discrimination; an inclination to serve; the joys and lessons of motherhood; physical grace and beauty, and a wonderful ability to laugh and weep. These may be some of the most important advantages to a Spiritual journey. Rest assured that every Soul is treated individually and given all that Its capacity can handle, regardless of gender, race, sexual preference, or other meaningless classifications.

I do not mean to suggest that women should be placed ahead of men, only that they should never be placed behind. Does anyone think that the Holy Power is sexist? For those engaged in the war between the sexes, be advised: one will frequently be switching sides.

It does not matter if one is getting along with their family. Like the infamous cowbird, who lays its eggs in other birds' nests, thus insuring their young are raised by complete strangers of a different species, evolved Souls are often deposited among totally dysfunctional families that are far behind them in evolution.

They are there to help while simultaneously experiencing the common trials of human life; the understanding gained from such experience prepares them for their mission; much friction is needed to polish a diamond, and it must endure many "cuts" before attaining the proper form that will most effectively channel the "Light."

Buddha left his wife and child; Jesus disowned his family when they tried to stop him from preaching, claiming He was "beside himself," a particularly ironic translation since it was probably true in a Spiritual sense, He, running His body from outside it. Of course, family is important, very important, but one's relationship with God is infinitely more important.

Jesus said "that a man's foes shall be they of his own household," and that His family were those that did the "will of God." His religious affiliation? "the believers."

It does not matter if one has a master, guru, pope, priest, pastor, rabbi, Brahmin, monk, or any other Spiritual authority outside of oneself, as the Holy Spirit, the Divine Self, Atman,

Jiva, and the Human Soul are all inside oneself. One need not go anywhere else.

A true "master," as defined here, is a Soul that has established themselves in the positive God-Worlds. Such a one, as the Hindus correctly believe, would never claim to be a master, or ever permit being given a title, any title, which of course would make them near impossible to find. Why?

Because those in the higher worlds know that the human vehicle is not the master. They would not dare to give the impression that they in the human consciousness were the "doer." That kind of self-declaration is left to those on the fourth plane and lower who will sincerely claim the highest titles ever coined. Many lower teachers agree with this principle but when offered a title, usually by their followers, they cannot resist. Perhaps one of the greatest evils on this plane is the worship of the personality.

Furthermore, helpers from the higher positive God-Worlds are horrified, ashamed, and befuddled by aspects of their own human consciousness. Their Human Soul and mind know this and are doing all it can do to apply and follow what it has been shown: of course, there is a balance of success and failure, and that woman down the block who is a full-fledged master may appear as a basket case at times.

Paramatman; the Holy Word; the Christ Self; the Spirit of God; the Divine Self; the Audible Sound Current; this is the Master. For the human vehicle to claim that it is a master, or agree to a title, is anathema to those so involved, and many consider such claims treasonous by those in a human body, or any other body. The Christ within Jesus stated: "Neither be ye called masters: for one is your Master, even Christ."

I do not mean to impugn "Souls" from the God-Worlds who are genuine masters, as their help and protection, if obtained, are priceless! I say, "if obtained," since few masters want followers or students, whether they have a body on Earth or not; it would depend on their mission. However, be assured, there are legions of legitimate helpers at every level on the "other side" just looking for Souls to help, teach, assist, protect and love.

In addition, there are teachers and helpers on Earth who are lower than masters but still credible as instructors and taught aspirants who can help teach and explain the principles of life. However, the whole business is a minefield, and one best be led by the Holy Force if they are looking for a teacher, as many are corrupt to the core.

The ones performing unconsciously are the worst, as they may appear the most sincere. It is usually true that they do not know what they are talking about, offering false promises and fear for money. God bless the exceptions, and God bless those who are not; they are both needed and have their place under the Sun. The way to God is simple. Learn to recognize your Higher Self's voice, and follow It through sincere trial and error; Self-direction is the goal in God's great school of life.

www.ingramcontent.com/pod-product-compliance
Lightning Source LLC
Chambersburg PA
CBHW071442070526
44578CB00001B/189